Aug. 14, 2015

To KA

Thank you so much for your support! May God continue to bless you and your school year!

Best Regards,

Walter Lee Porter

The Greatness Within

How to Manage PEACE in Your Life

Walter Lee Prater

authorHOUSE®

AuthorHouse™
1663 Liberty Drive
Bloomington, IN 47403
www.authorhouse.com
Phone: 1 (800) 839-8640

© 2015 Walter Lee Prater. All rights reserved.

No part of this book may be reproduced, stored in a retrieval system, or
transmitted by any means without the written permission of the author.

Published by AuthorHouse 02/18/2015

ISBN: 978-1-4969-6787-9 (sc)
ISBN: 978-1-4969-6795-4 (hc)
ISBN: 978-1-4969-6789-3 (e)

Print information available on the last page.

Any people depicted in stock imagery provided by Thinkstock are models,
and such images are being used for illustrative purposes only.
Certain stock imagery © Thinkstock.

This book is printed on acid-free paper.

Because of the dynamic nature of the Internet, any web addresses or links contained in
this book may have changed since publication and may no longer be valid. The views
expressed in this work are solely those of the author and do not necessarily reflect the views
of the publisher, and the publisher hereby disclaims any responsibility for them.

Tabel of Contents

The Origin 1

The Journey 3

Mastering Your True Self 5

January — Accepting The Past 7

February — The Educational Foundation 25

March — The Real You 41

April — Maintaining Health 59

Mastering Your Connections 75

May — Family Ties 77

June — The World Around You 95

July — Managing Relationships 111

August — Building Wealth 129

Mastering Your Power 147

September — The Gift Of Now 149

October — Discovering Purpose 165

November — The Pursuit Of Happiness 183

December — Constructing Your Future 199

The Truth 217

To Millie, for her unconditional
love and support
To Ruby Lee, for her motherly
sacrifices and inspiration
To Charles Durden, for his fatherly
wisdom and reassurance
To the Logan-Prater nation, for
demonstrating the power of family
To friends, old and new, for their
timely moments of encouragement
And to everyone who has decided
to live the best life imaginable
This volume is respectfully dedicated.

THE ORIGIN

Chaos in the world, as we know it, is built on the lie that everything that we need to be successful is outside of us. We are told that if we do not have particular brands of products, exquisite services or certain types of relationships, we are bound to have an unsuccessful life. For those people that believe in such a lie, they have an emptiness inside of them because their peace is dependent upon acquiring the things that they have been told will bring them closer to success.

This mentality serves as the backbone of greed, oppression and violence when left untreated. We live in such a world that technology has flourished, while our humanity has diminished. We are much more connected, but have much fewer relationships. We give praise to potential alone instead of accomplished deeds. We look toward everyone else for the answers and never consider trusting ourselves. We are shackled by the illusions that we enjoy the most and freely give our power away. This is not the way our lives were meant to be lived.

The only way for us to fill this void is to restore peace in our lives. Peace is commonly defined as pure tranquility and freedom from disturbance. Peace exists when we learn and apply principles that bring harmony and balance to our lives. The most interesting quality about peace is that no matter the circumstances, we still have the power to live a life of serenity. The ultimate question is ***"How do we manage living our best lives with inner peace?"*** The answer – *by examining and developing the greatness within us.*

THE JOURNEY

THE GREATNESS WITHIN teaches applicable life lessons and techniques that encourage **PEACE – the highest achievement of truth attainable in life.** The better we manage these techniques, the more consistent experiences of PEACE will be expressed in our lives.

We are embarking on a journey that will reveal the truth of who we are. This is not a moment of chance or coincidence. In life, we all struggle with some type of challenge. Addictions, offensive treatment of others and trouble coping with turmoil only scratch the surface of what we may endure. But there is always hope. Even in the loneliest of hours and darkest of circumstances, we are capable of having peace in our lives by developing our personal philosophy to strengthen our innermost being. We may not be perfect, but we can always be better.

In the spirit of personal advancement, guidance is given regarding some of life's most commonly asked questions, such as: *"What career path should I pursue?"*, *"What is my purpose?"* and *"What actions do I take to live the best life possible?"* This volume will also provide various practices for better living, such as how to:

- Accept the shortcomings of our past
- Respectfully resolve conflict
- Improve self-esteem and confidence
- Cope with disappointment
- Become wealthy in every aspect of life
- Foster productive relationships

As participants in humanity, it is our responsibility to honor our past, be productive in our present and bring about a more peaceful world for the future – our children. To achieve these goals, we must focus on the inner peace of the individual. World Peace begins in you. The primary task is to understand and cultivate your philosophy for a peaceful and productive existence. Your development centers on the mastery of three areas: Your True Self, Your Connections and Your Power. The application of the teachings in this volume is key to empowered living.

MASTERING YOUR TRUE SELF

The first stage of pursuing peace is all about you. This begins with considering how your past has affected you and then highlights some of the life principles that a successful foundation is built upon. Before you can have an understanding of everything around you, you must know yourself in the purest form. The module ends with valuable information on how to maintain yourself and your valuable resources. Together, these ideas are designed to strengthen your self-confidence.

JANUARY

ACCEPTING THE PAST

From grand events to the smallest details, our history has shaped who we are today. The majority of the personal issues that we may face will stem from a past disappointment or trauma. We must view our history through the eyes of motivation so that it fuels our desires instead of dismantling them. It is critical to accept the past because if we do not, we will be forever shackled by it.

JANUARY 1

YOUTH
The time in life between childhood & adulthood

Major moments of our youth shape who we are today. Unfortunately, a vault of negativity can open as a result. Look at the past for what it is - a time that was and is now gone. Nothing will ever change the past. Use your past only as current motivation. To relive the pain and agony of the past only holds us back from seeing the wonderful things that life has in store for us. Press through the pain, no matter what the source. Those situations become the moments that we can forever cherish because they will ignite the determination within us to improve our circumstances. This is how you overcome your past.

To embrace your past is the first step on the path to a better tomorrow.

JANUARY 2

HISTORY
Chronological record of significant events

One day, I asked my world history teacher "Why is knowing history so important? Am I ever going to use this?" With a half-smile on his face, my teacher replied, "Keep living. One day you will understand." Soon enough, the day of enlightenment came. While researching the goals I wanted to accomplish in my life, I realized a subtle yet amazing fact. I found myself looking into the history of successful people to learn what they did (and did not do) to be successful. The key is to create an outline to pattern your actions so you can better the chances for achievement.

Understand history to receive timesaving wisdom.

JANUARY 3

RECTIFY
To correct or make right

No matter what the age, we all can create a clean slate from conflict in a couple of ways. One way is to agree to disagree when reaching a 'breaking point' with another. This is quite effective at resolving issues because at the least, both sides have their moment to give their perspective. A second way is to inform the person of the wrong thought or action committed and then let it go. If the person understands the fault, then all is well. If the person refuses to understand, at least you can know what to expect from them in the future. Keep moving forward.

The unresolved issue is the beginning of a new problem.

JANUARY 4

REVERENCE
A feeling or attitude of deep respect

We all know people that shaped who we are and what we do with our lives. These people dedicated countless amounts of time to their work hoping to pass the torch to us so we could be successful. Remember the sacrifices of those before you. In most cases, they gave their blood, sweat and tears so you would not need suffer. Know that you did not achieve the goal by yourself when you are praised. Think of the people who were trailblazers in your field or those who took the time to teach you what you needed to reach your goals. Leave something positive and substantial for those who will follow in your footsteps to continue the legacy.

Always give honor to the people whose shoulders you stand upon.

JANUARY 5

CLARITY
Easy to understand or clear in appearance

With any goals, distinct pictures reside in our minds of what we expect to accomplish. If you possess the skills, resources and the opportunity to seize a moment, then focus and perform. Be direct with what you are attempting to do and seek help from experts along the way. They will hold valuable information for you to guide you to what you desire.

Understanding the road conditions will give you a quick & safe passage to your destination.

JANUARY 6

VULNERABLE
Open to attack, criticism or temptation

We are conditioned to believe that negative things are bound to happen to us, but this is not true. Life will throw major challenges at us but we cannot be overcome with fear. Regardless of how strong or weak we perceive ourselves to be, we are in control of the life bestowed onto us. Never be afraid to seek and embrace good experiences. We must trust our thoughts and actions as we work toward positive things so we will not miss out on great experiences that will come our way.

Do not allow fear to corner you as a victim.

JANUARY 7

RELEASE
To let go of a stronghold

We all encounter moments when we realize that some people expect us to fail. These people are the same ones who tell you what you cannot do because they do not believe they can have success. How often do we base our abilities on someone else's experience? Abandon the limitations that others place on you. Discard all wasteful energy and push toward your goals with what remains.

Cast away all that does not benefit you.

JANUARY 8

RECONCILE
To re-establish a relationship

Take the opportunity to re-establish a once fruitful relationship and to appreciate the importance of strong support systems. Some of these individuals can give us an encouraging word or a listening ear so we can move on with the tasks in front of us. We tend to take these relationships for granted as life progresses. Simple lacks of communication can damage any relationship. Do you know of any long, lost friends or family you could contact? A couple of phone calls can go a long way.

People who do not value relationships are soon left with none.

JANUARY 9

YESTERDAY
A day ago or recent past

Negative situations of our past seem to burn their way into the pits of our emotions. Sure, some "bad" experiences may occur, but we choose whether to take those negative emotions with us or not. Life gives us various types of experiences and what we choose to hold on to will have lasting effects. It is not always easy, we must put forth the effort to separate the joy (positive) and the lesson (negative) from all experiences to be productive. Do not take life's bitter moments into fresh experiences.

Keep the important pieces of yesterday that will carry you through tomorrow.

JANUARY 10

HUMILITY
Moderate opinion of one's value, achievements and abilities

You may encounter people who are talented and well known. Some of them tend to believe they are so much better than others. To experience true and lasting success, one must be humble. Humble people center themselves in respecting others and investing into their work ethic. Being humble is not about thinking people are beneath you in any way. Humility is not weakness - it is a lasting sign of internal strength.

Success is granted only to those humble enough to receive it.

JANUARY 11

ACCOUNTABILITY
To accept responsibility for one's actions

No one can ever "make" you do anything. As the classic question about peer pressure goes, "If someone tells you to jump off a bridge, are you going to do it?" For any request made before us, we have the power and the right to say no. On the other side of the coin, we also must accept full responsibility for our actions. The decision always rests in our hands.

YOU are the only person responsible for YOUR actions.

JANUARY 12

INTENSITY
Exceptional concentration, power or force

Does a person's power exist in a resoundingly loud space? No. Is one's power comprised of uncontrolled movement? Absolutely not. Brash noise and lack of control does not make a person powerful. To be intense is to exhibit complete focus on a task coupled with controlled, direct action. This is the key to all work toward accomplishing tasks. The more centered one's mental and physical energy is, the higher the likelihood of achieving the goal.

Intense preparation leads to a high-level of performance.

JANUARY 13

ZERO
Complete absence of value; to possess nothing

Starting from scratch is quite the challenge. The new beginning occurs as a new set of circumstances or the result of a substantial loss. Instead of viewing this as a sad or negative point in life, look at it as an opportunity for a fresh start to work toward a better life. It may take time but you already have the most important asset - yourself.

Starting over gives you the power to author a new and exciting chapter of your life.

JANUARY 14

DEFEAT
Failure to accomplish a desired goal

The risk of failure is present every time we attempt a goal. We may work harder, study harder or even practice more than everyone else does but the chance remains that we may not attain the success we want. Nevertheless, no matter how horrible the failure may seem, teachable moments will arise. In these instances, you can learn more about the overall experience, correct your mistakes and improve yourself. Failure inspires critical development much more than winning does.

Each defeat is worth the agony when you embrace the lesson along the way.

JANUARY 15

LOGIC
Chronological record of significant events

People are creatures of habit. If we constantly find ourselves in tough or compromising situations, consider the choices we made to affect our negative condition. Our decisions retain the power to affect today, next month and even next year. If a trend appears which seems unfavorable to you, explore how you can avoid such anguish by choosing to move in a different direction.

If your shoes are hurting your feet, put on a different pair.

JANUARY 16

TRUTH
That which is actual or in accordance with fact and reality

People will tell you anything to persuade you to do what they want. The majority of your decisions are based on information from others, so you must confirm the information is truly based on fact. You must do your best to prove all things so your judgment is sound. Society often operates based on what the majority of people think, without regard to whether the idea is true or not. Successful people make decisions on that which is known, not by what the masses may feel or think on a random day. Truth is the foundation of all information and all virtues. You own the strength to choose concepts of proven truth instead of following meaningless opinions supported my misled people.

Although an idea may be popularly accepted, that does not mean that it is true.

JANUARY 17

LOSS
Feeling of grief when deprived of someone or something of value

Some of our most pivotal moments revolve around a loss. The deficiency of resources, ability or even people can be tough to manage within the situation. It is easy to fall into a mentality of worthlessness and self-pity. Instead of going down this slippery slope, pour your energy into what remains. Our most creative moments occur when we lack resources because genius is born out of necessity. Take the remaining pieces of a broken situation and explore how they can evolve into magnificent opportunities.

Do not worry about what was lost, but cherish what you have left.

JANUARY 18

ATTENDANCE
Frequency that a person is present

Your participation in any event is important. For example, the moment a celebrity enters a restaurant for a meal, an electricity buzzes within the establishment from the excitement. You do not need to be a celebrity to create these effects. You possess a unique energy within your own skills and personality. Fantastic opportunities can arise when you simply show up.

You instantly add value to the room when you arrive.

JANUARY 19

CREATIVITY
Ability & power to create; characterized by
originality and expressiveness

Society will pressure you to conform to others to exhibit the same habits, same appearance and even the same type of life. Every advancement in history occurred due to someone taking a stand and daring to do something against the norm. Trust your creativity and express yourself honestly to push the envelope of plain thought.

*Your contribution to the beauty in the world
is extremely valuable.*

JANUARY 20

AUTHORITY
Power to influence or enforce

In all roles, a hierarchy exists of who is in charge of various tasks. The fool would attempt to move quickly and recklessly up the ladder without regard to those involved. This wastes time and energy. The wise would look strive do the best job possible in the current role while networking with others to market what they are capable of doing. The opportunities will present themselves and these key people will place candidates at the top of the list who can follow directions the best.

Power and respect are gained only by yielding to those in charge.

JANUARY 21

DISTRACTION
An interruption or obstacle to concentration

On all journeys toward a worthy end, some factors will attempt to take your energy away from the task. People are definitely in this category, but surprisingly, the biggest distractions are ourselves. Sometimes, we get in our own way to hinder the achievement of a goal by yielding to fear and doubt. Remind yourself of the most motivating reason to achieve the task if the challenging winds blow you off course.

Distractions will arrive, so keep your purpose in mind.

JANUARY 22

IGNORANCE
Lack of knowledge, information or education

It is often believed that the ignorant are the most happy. Those working toward this type of bliss are traveling a road of emptiness and mediocrity. What you do not know, can hurt you. You are not equipped to reach a goal if you do not know what is required of you. The movers and shakers of the world know that if you are aware of your current limitations, then you have a target to reach - an end to pursue. Open yourself to unexplored ideas and experiences or be left on an island of regret.

You may not have all of the answers but you will be responsible in searching for them.

JANUARY 23

MEDITATION
An act yielding mental calmness and physical relaxation

In some moments, life will get the best of us. We will struggle to balance family obligations, work, relationships and an assortment of other tasks. When you reach the boiling point, get away for a while. Find a quiet location where you can sit comfortably still and focus on the sound of your deep, strong breaths. Relax each muscle from the sole of your feet to the crown of your head. This simple act gives the mind a moment to renew and refresh itself for what comes next.

Take a few moments alone to focus on what absolutely matters - breathing.

JANUARY 24

CHARACTER
Combination of qualities portraying moral excellence and firmness

A challenge is the only mechanism to expose the truth of our character. If you genuinely want to learn about the character of people, find the moments when they were pushed with their backs against the wall and watch how they responded. The key to maintaining a good character is to make solid, consistent choices so goodness and truth can be expected from you.

Who are you when no one is watching?

JANUARY 25

QUALITY
A distinguishing attribute; superiority in kind

Time is always of the essence and there is much work to be done. This creates urgency for making sure the quality of our work is of a high standard the first time we complete the tasks. If someone tries to finish the work quickly and makes many mistakes, how productive is the worker? More time would be wasted making avoidable corrections. The finished work is the direct representative of the person.

What does your work say about you?

JANUARY 26

APATHY
Lack of interest or concern

Many people do not fill their lives with passion because of past disappointments. They are convinced they have seen it all and there is nothing worthwhile beyond their current circumstances. Do not be one of these people. There is much more to life than current situations. Your future is much brighter than what happened in your past. Take an active role in your life by taking the lead. Initiate experiences instead of waiting for them to happen. Nothing will just fall into your lap.

If you show no zest for life, it will not give you the joy you seek.

JANUARY 27

BETRAYAL
To fail or desert in the time of need

People can be so selfish that they knowingly betray you to get what they want. It is easy to hold a grudge and be angry at them for their actions. In order to move past the betrayal, you must separate the emotion from the situation. Fully accept their selfish thinking so you can recognize exactly what to expect from them the next time. This valuable information will help you to make a better decision based on who is truly in your corner supporting you and who is not.

When people burn you, take away their matches.

JANUARY 28

COMFORT
A satisfying of enjoyable experience

We all wish success came easily. A major factor that causes people to stop the pursuit of a worthy goal is the perceived difficulty. These so-called difficult moments arise not to punish us, but they appear as an opportunity to learn. You must recognize what is required of you to perform at the level necessary to achieve the goal. Learn to be comfortable with uncomfortable situations.

To walk into greatness you must step out of your comfort zone.

JANUARY 29

SUCCESS
A favorable or desired outcome; the attainment of favor or wealth

Most people assume success is when the overall achievement is reached, but this not true. When climbing the mountain of a goal, success is determined by the phases reached. Along the way, you can look back, assess the progress and confirm the positive direction of your movement. The smaller accomplishments serve as motivation toward the next stage.

All past accomplishments are fuel
for overcoming current challenges.

JANUARY 30

INITIATIVE
At one's own discretion; independent of outside influence or control

These days, we are all busy. We are pulled in many directions at the same time so we must be efficient with all of our resources. To reduce the length of our task list, we must complete as much work as we can with high-quality results. We often put off work until later but the people who shape the world do not wait until just before the deadline to begin the work. They finish well in advance of the deadline to correct any mistakes and make improvements to the final product.

If you know what needs to be done, do not wait - DO IT.

JANUARY 31

LIBERATION
Complete freedom from all restraints, confinement or bondage

The world will try to put all types of limits on you. Some people will tell you that you are not good enough to achieve your goals. Others will discourage you and say you are wasting your time. People will criticize your every step because they do not believe they can do anything worthwhile. Never live in the box people will try to place you in. Focus on your education, your performance and, most importantly, your purpose. This practice frees you from the negativity that the world will throw in your direction.

There is no opponent.

FEBRUARY

THE EDUCATIONAL FOUNDATION

There are basic aspects of life that make each day much easier to manage when properly applied. These natural principles are entrenched within our daily lives, although they may go unnoticed. The fundamentals of successful living are not secrets for the elite or privileged. One must understand life's universal principles to navigate toward success.

FEBRUARY 1

QUESTION
A sentence worded or expressed to elicit information

As we learn about life and our place in the world, we must ask questions about all things that affect our lives. Questions are the mallet and chisel used to remove meaningless material from the jewels of truth we seek. Any hindrance to unveiling the truth will waste much of our resources, which leaves us with nothing gained. There is neither time nor energy to waste. At the same time, if we are not receiving the answers we seek, we are asking the wrong questions.

Claim your right to question everything.

FEBRUARY 2

EFFORT
A vigorous or determined attempt

In this life, I found myself many times saying that I did not do something because of others. Those people used discouraging words or even ridiculed me to paint the picture of how "impossible" my goal was and sometimes, I listened. Soon enough, I realized the problem was not them – the issue was with me. Rather than focusing on how excellent my tools were, I was terrified by the height of the mountain. After some time of frustration, I realized a profound truth. There is only one thing a person is in complete control of in this world – effort. There is absolutely nothing anyone can say or do to affect how much effort I invest into a goal. No one else can control my determination, my focus and, most importantly, my sweat. I began to maximize all I could control and my desired results were soon to follow.

The magnitude of your effort will determine your results.

FEBRUARY 3

COMMITMENT
The act of pledging or engaging oneself

Commitment is all about doing what you say you are going to do. When you follows-through on what you have spoken, the reliability of your word is strengthened. It gives people confidence to know that they can count on you completing your assigned task. An inner strength shines when you know how to work through challenging times and finish what you start. Your value increases since such a trait is hard to find in people these days.

Our commitments announce to the world who we are.

FEBRUARY 4

UNDERSTANDING
Sympathetically aware of other people's feelings

With all of the experiences life can present, you must know how to relate to people. This does not mean to avoid speaking the truth to people. Listen to their side of the story to get an idea of their perspective. Once you know this, you can decide for yourself what you would do in such a situation and give them helpful insight to manage the issue. Your words could be just what they needed to inspire them toward positive results.

One of the most valuable asset of communication is knowing how to try on someone else's shoes.

FEBRUARY 5

FUNDAMENTALS
A central rule or principle on which something is based

The most challenging subject matters begin as a single idea, just as every procedure is nothing more than a series of small steps. These ideas and steps are the building blocks which can become complex as more are added. The fundamentals are the basic knowledge and skills required to perform a task. Do not allow yourself to be overwhelmed into thinking that something is too difficult to do. The overall task becomes easier to complete when you divide the job into smaller pieces of work.

Even a tree of infinite knowledge has simple roots.

FEBRUARY 6

EDUCATION
The process of giving or receiving systematic instruction

Your education is something no one can take away. Knowledge alone does not guarantee success, yet it will expose more opportunities to you. When coupled with a strong, focused work ethic, an education can thrust you into favorable situations from which you can benefit. It can lead you into the right social circles for networking purposes or even inspire you to pursue a financially lucrative idea. In short, never underestimate the power of education.

Knowledge is the foundation of all achievements.

FEBRUARY 7

EXCELLENCE
The quality of being outstanding or extremely good

Most people are actually afraid of being successful. You would think success would be something everyone wants and would run toward, but that is not the case. Many are afraid of the new standard established. They feel that if they win now, they must win everything from today forward. Those who exhibit excellence are not at all concerned with this fear. Their belief is that there is no reason to perform a task unless you begin with the expectation of the highest level of results. To adopt this mental approach allows you to put in the work and energy to perform as closely to perfect as possible. When you expect greatness, great things will come to you.

*Always shoot for the moon so that if you fail,
you can still fall amongst the stars.*

FEBRUARY 8

FUNCTION
The role to be fulfilled by something that is designed

All creations around you hold a particular task to be fulfilled. They each may differ drastically and varying degrees of importance, but they all retain a common factor – they all declare purpose. People are the same way. We all possess attributes and skills, which make us unique, and we each have a positive purpose. We are not here for one reason alone. The fact we have life means we are open to explore our many purposes.

Everything in existence has purpose – including you.

FEBRUARY 9

RESEARCH

A systematic investigation to establish
facts and reach new conclusions

If you want to achieve an accomplishment, begin by finding all of the needed information. This is a great habit when there is an important decision in front of you. Look deeper into the matter to help you to make a sound decision. In addition, you can plan your steps more effectively and avoid pitfalls by studying those who were successful in your field and those who were not. You then can learn from real examples of successful habits and decisions which lead to failure.

*The more information in your possession,
the better quality decision you can make.*

FEBRUARY 10

HOPE

A feeling of expectation and desire for a certain thing to happen

Hope serves as the antidote to the despair of life. Without a positive outlook, our life force weakens. We become unproductive and depressed when our determination decreases. This is not how we are to live our lives. Hope is a choice – a belief of better days ahead. Neither minor nor dramatic inconveniences bother you. You easily maneuver around closed paths to find another way. Most importantly, you can positively inspire people all over the world.

*Hope is a common tool, but the decision is
yours to carry it with you or not.*

FEBRUARY 11

MASTER
One who has acquired extensive knowledge or skills in a given area

No one is born a master. To reach such an esteemed level takes time, information and opportunities for application. Successful people throughout the ages focused on an area to learn everything involved to make a living to sustain themselves and their families. They then applied what they learned by working within their craft to sharpen those skills. To become a master in your own right, you must find a passionate area in which to specialize so the time you invest practicing in your area can effortlessly pass.

If you become an expert in an area you enjoy, you never have to work a day in your life.

FEBRUARY 12

ASSISTANCE
The action of helping someone with a task

The spirit of helpfulness is a natural part of our humanity. Throughout our existence, we will need help of some type whether in the form of someone nursing us back to good health or helping us to learn challenging material. We must learn to be humble enough to ask for help and sincere enough to give the same whenever we see the need. Each of us has qualities and skills in various areas, which can benefit others. We commonly travel the same roads toward achievement, so it is wise to place the things you do not do well in the hands of someone who does.

Only the naive think success can be reached alone.

FEBRUARY 13

BREAKFAST

A meal eaten in the morning, the first of the day

Breakfast is the most important meal of the day. The initial meal helps to begin your day without the distraction of hunger, which makes you much more productive. Visualize what you want to happen throughout the day. Create the mental pictures and setup your strategy to maximize the time available for you to increase the likelihood of your success.

Be patient and enjoy your breakfast.
You have a full day ahead of you.

FEBRUARY 14

BOOKS

A written or printed work

The world's most precious resources are not oil and diamonds – they are books. Books can teach you life lessons for improvement or provide a much-needed escape from your hectic day. They can even cause you to become someone you never thought imaginable. Power resides in written expression. Words also have an inspirational quality that can end wars and turn lives around for the better. When you learn the true value of books, you hold all possibilities in your hands.

The wealth of the world is found in a book close to you.

FEBRUARY 15

IMAGINATION
The action forming new ideas not present to the senses

Imagination is rooted in making something out of nothing. To reach this magnificent feat, you must learn to visualize the possibilities of what you can see, do or become. The use of imagination empowers us to think beyond our current limitations to create something fresh and innovative. What could you create if the veil of boundaries were lifted? What would you do if all of your options were open?

All things begin their existence as a single picture in the mind.

FEBRUARY 16

CONSIDERATION
Careful thought, typically over a period of time

We are much more powerful than we think. Our actions affect the lives of those close to us in relationship and proximity. For this reason, we must be aware of ourselves so we do not intentionally cause harm to others. This does not mean to mask the truth to spare someone's feelings. It means to take responsibility for your words and your actions for use in the building up of humanity, not in its destruction.

Be sure your actions do not threaten the lives of others.

FEBRUARY 17

GOALS
The objective toward which effort is directed

What would you like to accomplish in your life? Is there a hobby you want to begin? What dream location would you like to visit? Each of these questions will prompt you to establish a goal. Simply put, a goal is anything you want to do or obtain. Surprisingly, the most important piece to this puzzle is not the goal itself, but the desire to achieve it. This desire gives you boldness and direction to experience something worthwhile. Such a spark ignites life's possibilities and exposes your determination to the world.

__Goal setting is the first action taken toward accomplishing a task.__

FEBRUARY 18

ANALYZE
To examine the methodology and detailed structure of

If a goal is the destination to reach, then the method used to analyze the situation determines your road map. What resources do you have? How much time do you need? Who has already completed the journey and in what direction did they travel? Questions such as these help you to assess your specific situation and create your detailed plan of action. Execute your plan well and revise the details as needed.

*__What is required to move you from where
you are to where you want to be?__*

FEBRUARY 19

ORGANIZATION
The arrangement of related or connected items

In a cluttered work area, how effectively can you work? It is difficult to find needed items when an area is not organized. This also is true about our ideas. In the early stages of learning, normally a bulk of information is introduced at one time, which can be overwhelming. Organize your ideas by segmenting them into related chunks to make them easier to manage.

Less time is wasted when resources are better organized.

FEBRUARY 20

TEST
A procedure intended to establish the quality, performance or reliability of something before being taken into widespread use.

Challenging moments will always occur. There is absolutely no way to avoid them. Make these situations easier to deal with by approaching each experience like a test. Each test is different, yet it will usually result in: 1) conquering a fear, 2) learning a lesson, or 3) developing your endurance. You will know you have passed the test when you are able to teach someone how to work though a similar situation.

Life's occasional tests are designed to extract greatness from you.

FEBRUARY 21

FACTS
Knowledge based on real or actual occurrences

Facts give you consistency. Opinions are based on feelings at a particular time. If you are building a foundation for a home, sand is not sturdy enough to handle the weight of a home. Use a concrete foundation instead to create a strong support to build the home. Important decisions are based on strong facts – ideas that have been proven with substantial evidence. You must be sure of your information because it helps you to minimize the number of things outside of your control.

Do not invest your energy into things that can change with the wind.

FEBRUARY 22

LEADERSHIP
The giving of guidance or direction

What does leadership look like? Should a leader focus on individual performance to lead by example? Leadership styles vary similar to our skills and attributes. Leadership lives in the decision to make a positive impact to benefit the group as a whole. In order to lead others, you must exhibit leadership qualities in your own life. Leaders make the tough choices which are sometimes unpopular, but for the best overall outcome. Trust your decisions to advance yourself and others will so the same.

Failure to act is the leading cause of the empty life.

FEBRUARY 23

PRESSURE
A compelling or hindering influence on the mind or will

People who wanted to justify the fear that paralyzed them and kept them from completing a task created the concept of "pressure". It is found in the moments where performance is the most critical to reaching success. Fear is not real – it is an illusion. Pressure is another form of fear. Therefore, pressure is also an illusion. Focus on the goal and the task to be completed. Do not be fearful of what "could" happen. That is a waste of your time and energy.

Pressure does not exist, so simply prepare and perform.

FEBRUARY 24

READ
To look at and understand the meaning of letters, words and symbols

Another way to grasp a different perspective is to read about ideas and the experiences of others. As you learn about various subject matters, your communication skills improve because reading naturally expands your vocabulary and cognitive ability. You will process information faster and be able to analyze deeper relationships within sets of data. Therefore, losing yourself in a newspaper article or a thrilling novel is very beneficial for your development.

The more you read the better you will express your thoughts.

FEBRUARY 25

BRAINSTORM

A spontaneous outpouring of thoughts used to produce
new ideas and methods of solving problems

A brainstorming session is an efficient way to gather many ideas in a relatively short period. Alone or in a group setting, you can use this method to figure out your objective, resources and your strategy. A think-tank such as this maximizes the experience and practical understanding of those involved. As everyone follows the moderator's lead, an abundance of ideas will flow.

*Allow the wellspring of your creativity
to thrust you into new dimensions.*

FEBRUARY 26

GIFTED

To possess exceptional talent or ability

We all are gifted in some aspect whether we are aware of the fact or not. This noble attribute comes with vast responsibility. You must not think your giftedness alone is enough to guarantee success for you. Many people are naturally talented yet have accomplished nothing because they lacked the drive to sacrifice for success. If this describes you, remember, there has never been an expiration date on success. Start now.

*The gifted one and the lazy one can
both suffer from the same symptoms.*

FEBRUARY 27

MEMORY
To recall or recognize facts or previous experiences

The importance of memories is misunderstood quite often. The memories can be positive or negative yet both help to advance our development. Positive memories give us hope for the future and serve as a reminder of the good choices we make. Negative memories always involve a lesson to be learned which is ultimately for our benefit. Every aspect of our past, whether we believed the experience was good or bad, was to make us better.

Use your memories to motivate you toward a positive direction.

FEBRUARY 28

ANSWERS
A spoken or written reply to a question

What would make my life better? What goals to I want to accomplish? Am I truly giving everything I can to succeed? What is my purpose in life? Major life questions will arise often and it is good to get insight from a trusted, knowledgeable person. Seeking wisdom from others is beneficial to you but may be based purely on the advisor's perspective. At the end of the day, the decision or task rests on you. With time, you will be able to realize there is only one person who has the answers.

The answers to life's most challenging questions are found in front of the mirror.

FEBRUARY 29

INSPIRATION

The process of being mentally stimulated to do or feel something

Inspiration exists in different forms. It can reside in the laughter of a child, a brilliant work of art or in the idea of winning a championship. It is also a major piece needed to put together the puzzle of your dreams. Your inspiration is the reason why you are willing to risk blood, sweat and tears to accomplish your desired task. You must search deeply to find this driving force. The good are able to <u>find</u> inspiration, but the extraordinary have learned how to <u>create</u> it. With that in mind, what is your reason?

On the rocky road of your learning curve, focus on your inspiration to carry you through the twists & turns.

MARCH

THE REAL YOU

When you strip yourself of all masks and pretenses, who is left? In a world of various characters, the masses have been mistakenly taught that conforming to the expectations of others will ensure success. Very few people have the strength to be themselves. Veils are not necessary – authenticity is. Define yourself by the quality and application of your personal truth.

MARCH 1

NAME

A word or set of words by which a person, animal, place, or thing is identified, addressed or referred to.

Though we are given our name at birth, the value associated with the name lies in our hands. Our actions determine the impression people have when our name is mentioned. The next time you enter a room, notice the people's reactions. Is the response pleasant? Are they excited or do they become angry? This is important to recognize because those people may hold the keys of opportunities for you. The power of your name can improve your current conditions.

All you truly possess in this world is your name and your word, so, guard them well.

MARCH 2

VISION

The act or power of anticipating that which will or may come to be.

One of the most disappointing moments is to interact with someone who has no vision. We are people created with purpose in mind. Our lives always should illustrate a task to be done, a goal to accomplish or the life we want to live. Some may call you a dreamer and tell you to get your head out of the clouds. Remind them that this is where your greatness is born, and you must continue. Not everyone will be able to handle the magnitude of your vision. Times will come when you must keep your vision to yourself and allow others to only see the fruits of your work. You are never given a vision without having the ability to execute the task.

You must paint a mental picture of what you want for your goals to become a reality.

MARCH 3

RESPONSIBILITY

The state or fact of being accountable or to blame for something

It is important to know what people are responsible for because if you do not get the expected results, someone must be held accountable. A well-organized project will designate specific people to be in charge of a task to maximize their skill set. Do not seek glory for fulfilling your duty. You own a natural responsibility to improve everything in which you contact. Each of us has skills to maximize so that we contribute well to society.

Never seek credit for something you are supposed to do.

MARCH 4

REPUTATION

Beliefs or opinions held about someone or something in general

Do not worry about the opinions of others when you are doing what you know is right. People will say whatever they want to say anyway. Do not be concerned because the same people who praise you and put you on a pedestal may talk down upon you when challenging times occur. Be confident to know you are doing the right things.

People may speak negatively about you even when you are headed in a positive direction.

MARCH 5

BEAUTY

*A combination of qualities with the purpose of
pleasing the intellect or moral sense*

With all of the chaos in life, you must take a minute to enjoy the beautiful pieces of the experience. Enjoy a peaceful walk, tasting your favorite dessert or spending time with loved ones to take in life's pleasantries. These moments give you balance when we are in the midst of challenging times. You may see beauty in listening to positive genres of music or viewing artwork. In all things of beauty, you will find a common link – inspiration.

***Recognize the moments to witness the
beauty in people and situations.***

MARCH 6

OASIS

*A pleasant or peaceful area or period in the midst
of difficulty or a troubled situation*

Every so often, we must getaway and regroup. This escape can be a physical movement or simply a mental voyage away from a hectic day. As we work toward our goals, we eventually will drain our battery of motivation and must be recharged. The purpose of having your oasis is to have a place where you can be free of all the stresses and obligations. The more frequently you visit this land of tranquility, the more you learn how to manage the stressful cause.

Make time for rest and refreshment to replenish your soul.

MARCH 7

JOY
A sense of strong pleasure and happiness

In what areas do you experience joy? Some people encounter such delight when they interact with certain people. Others experience this bliss when they are doing an activity they love. The common factor is the joy driven by your passion. Can the direction of your passion be controlled? The answer is definitely. Do what you love and love what you do. You are in the driver's seat.

Your joy cannot be eliminated by anyone or anything.

MARCH 8

LIMITATIONS
A restricting rule or circumstance

People will do all they can to convince you of all of the limits you face. They will tell you how each lofty idea is unattainable, but there is no such thing as impossible. There is always more than one way to achieve your desires. Therefore, limits do not actually exist. The only difference between what you can and cannot do is the time you spend working toward the goal. Detours can still lead you to your destination.

You can only hit the wall if you are aiming for it.

MARCH 9

FAITH
Complete trust or confidence in someone or something

You must believe you are capable of achieving the specific goal you have dreamt of for years. Every moment of work you invest will pay off. You must believe no matter what comes in your way you will find a way over, under, around or through it. There is absolutely nothing that can stop you. The faith in yourself must always be greater than your faith in others.

If you do not believe in yourself, how do you expect others to believe in you?

MARCH 10

TEMPTATION
Something that seduces or has the quality to seduce

Temptations come in all shapes and sizes. To make the right choices is important but the challenge only begins here. You will also be tempted by laziness. Some days, you may not "feel" like working hard because you are already tired. You may even think if someone else is taking shortcuts you should be able to do the same. There is, however, only one road to success and it is paved with sweat, hard work and efficient planning.

The best outcomes are the offspring of tough choices.

MARCH 11

RELIABILITY
The quality of being dependable

Opportunities are most often granted to people known to follow through with tasks. People will have no problem assigning you important task tasks when they observe your reliability. The main factor in such situations is trust. Complete each job given to you within the allotted time and with the highest quality. As the responsibilities bestowed upon you increase, such a gesture shows people that are also increasing their confidence in you.

What good is your word if you do not honor it?

MARCH 12

INVENTORY
A tally of one's personality traits, aptitudes and skills

Every so often, it is wise to take an inventory of where you are and what you have. To question your education, a tedious project or simply your stance in life, serves as a powerful snapshot to help you reach goals. By taking this brief intermission, you can coordinate your efforts to fill in potential gaps appearing in your plan.

Taking self-inventory will expand your resources and opportunities.

MARCH 13

SOLITUDE
The state of being alone

A natural sense of peace exists when we are alone. You are most able to think clearly without distractions. You can work without interruption as well. In addition, you are able to make focused decisions without unproductive outside influences. In these moments, critical planning occurs to set yourself up for the next important move.

There is ultimate power in being the only one.

MARCH 14

TEARS
Indicators of strong happiness or sadness

Sometimes, life will present negative events our way that will seem to break us down. There is nothing at all wrong with crying – it purifies the soul. After our tears have been wiped away, we must remember to consider the conditions that we must change or learn to cope with so that we can move forward. Tears alone never initiate any monumental idea, nor execute any actions toward accomplishing a desired end. They serve to cleanse the well of your emotions to help you to focus in on your next step to achievement.

Your tears are never as effective as your sweat.

MARCH 15

MISTAKES
A misguided or wrong action or judgment

We all make mistakes whether they are honest mistakes or deliberate. Despite the type, it is still the shortcoming in decision-making. The good thing about them is that we can correct our actions. There is always an instance of a learning opportunity within the framework of our faulty decisions. We must find the error and correct ourselves, so we do not have to retake the test.

Mistakes cause more regret when you do not correct the fault.

MARCH 16

PERCEPTION
The state of being or process of becoming aware of something

Seek information from people and pay close attention to the base of their perspective. Do not allow people's negative experiences to discourage you from achievement. At the same time, do not become hypnotized into thinking someone's positive experience will automatically happen to you. Take in their experience for wisdom's sake, but allow your own experiences to unfold so you can establish your own perspective.

Be careful of the pictures people will paint before you.

MARCH 17

GRACE
Simple elegance or refinement of movement

Grace is exhibited as being smooth and fluid in movement. At times, the actions can seem effortless. Those who are confident in their skills and preparedness reach the point where they can move forward knowing their decision is the correct one. Grace is a quality available to all of us but used by a relative few.

Always strive to conduct yourself with grace and class.

MARCH 18

CONFORMITY
Behavior in accordance with socially accepted conventions or standards

It is good to pay attention to what the crowd is doing but do not assume you are bound to follow. In some cases, it may actually be good to follow if you see the obvious benefit. You, however, must trust your own decision-making to step away from the crowd and pursue what you believe is right or best. Some of the most pivotal decisions to affect your life positively may also be the most unpopular. You must move on.

Knowing when to join in with and when to separate from the crowd is a valuable gift.

MARCH 19

INTENTION
A planned end or aim

You must decide what you want to do, gather your resources, and move with purpose without hesitation. Major accomplishments are always a product of your decision to do something coupled with the actions needed to complete the task. Find a purpose for the benefit of society and the doors of assistance will open.

Your actions are more effective when they are founded with good intentions.

MARCH 20

STRENGTH
The quality or state of being mentally or physically withstanding of an opposing force

What does strength to look like? Some believe that the strongest people are those who may voice their opinion the loudest or be the most physical, but this not true. Those who are strong know what they are capable of and are not swayed by other people's opinions. They concern themselves with the development and success of others to show people the truth of their own inner strength.

True strength is not showing off your own ability, but managing the power of others.

MARCH 21

CONSCIENCE

*An inner sense or voice viewed as a guide to
the rightness or wrongness of one's behavior*

When we were young, we learned the difference between right and wrong. This was consistent as we grew into adulthood. Our conscience serves as an indicator to remind us of what is good and bad behavior. If I want to produce an apple tree, I must first plant the apple seed. Life works the same way. To receive good things in my life, I must perform good actions, which begin as good thoughts.

*After making a mistake, you can still
make the necessary corrections.*

MARCH 22

STATUS

*The position of an individual in relation to another or others,
especially in regard to social or professional standing*

In the pursuit of achievement, some people view their success by reflecting on the titles. Be careful not to let your title become more important than your name. One is simply what you do, while the other is who you are. If you place all of your value in your title, what would happen if the designation is removed for some reason? Do you cease to be who you are? No. Does your value decrease? No. Obtain your title so people know what to do, but always remember to be yourself.

Do not allow titles to inflate your pride and ego.

MARCH 23

CAPACITY

The maximum amount something can perform, yield, or withstand

It is easy to become overwhelmed when facing difficult times. These moments have purpose. In order for you to learn how much you can handle, you must experience trials. Life brings all types of challenging situations to your doorstep. Each of these challenges will help you realize what you are capable of and teach you how to conduct yourself properly.

You can only know your limits by being pushed to them.

MARCH 24

LOVE

An intense fondness of deep affection

Love is the strongest of all human emotions and is the only one to transcend all boundaries. Love does not allow foolishness nor accepts laziness. Love invokes a reason to take action, step out of your comfort zone and even to risk everything for the object of your affection. It can make us laugh and can make us cry, yet our existence is always better because of it.

Life is much more fulfilling when love is your motivation.

MARCH 25

INSTINCT
A natural or intuitive way of acting or thinking

We all are equipped with a mechanism to indicate what we should do and when we should do it. How often do we face choices and second-guess ourselves by overanalyzing the situation? At times, we end up making a less beneficial decision for ourselves. You must trust your gut instinct. There is no such thing as coincidence. Your instincts are intended to point you in the right direction. Master the balance of your intuition and your analytical processing to watch your decision-making drastically improve.

The first natural thought is usually the correct one.

MARCH 26

COURAGE
Strength in the face of pain or grief

To ignite your decision to act, you need a flammable base of courage. To be courageous does not mean the lack of fear. You must recognize how to move past the illusion of fear. Finding people who mastered this concept is not difficult at all. Ask someone about his or her defining moments. Most of these instances would involve moving past an empty fear to accomplish a goal, which takes courage. You control the ability to do the same. Most likely, you have already done it a number of times before but just need an occasional reminder.

Never be afraid to trust the greatness in you.

MARCH 27

DIGNITY

The state or quality of being worthy of honor or respect

Temptations to make bad choices are all around us in different forms. These choices usually involve misleading people from the ultimate truth, giving us an unfair advantage, or even causing harm to others. We must do our best to resist such temptations. We must strive to fill every moment with wholesome goodness, so we can continue to make the world a better place. No, we are not always perfect, but we do not need to yield to the pressure of society. You are always in charge of how you conduct your behavior.

Your actions in private are as important as those done in public.

MARCH 28

ATTITUDE

A settled way of thinking or feeling,
typically reflected in a person's behavior

Imagine the distance runner in his or her first marathon. Eventually fatigue will begin to affect how the runner performs. In the marathon of life, if we decide to stop at the first sign of discomfort, we will not grow beyond our current abilities. Life may be difficult at times, but as long as we keep running, we will reach the burst of energy of the "2nd wind". Maintain a positive outlook and move forward. Vast rewards will come.

*A positive attitude will carry you though
all challenging situations.*

MARCH 29

CONTROL

The power to direct people's behavior or the course of events

Accepting your current conditions can be very frustrating. The road toward the destination of your goal will uncover situations and decisions beyond your control. Remember to focus your energy into your resources and perform the actions that you are able to do. Everything else will work itself out in time.

Concern yourself only with the situations you can improve.

MARCH 30

STAND

A position taken in a particular issue or argument

With so many people in the world, we constantly face multiple options that people want us to support. Make the choice for yourself what is right for you to support after weighing all of the issues. No two people will agree on everything, so know that you are capable of deciding what is and what is not important to you. Once you have decided what you believe, stick to your word.

There is always an opportunity for you to stand up for what is right.

MARCH 31

ENSLAVEMENT
To reduce the rights of or subjugate

The road to success has many routes. You must determine what success looks like to you. If someone else wants you to become a doctor or lawyer, and you become one, that does not necessarily make you successful. You cannot base your achievement on someone else's goals. People who blindly follow the footsteps of others end up unhappy and unfulfilled because the goal was never theirs to pursue. For all that you invest your energy and resources into, be sure that goal is something you truly want do for yourself.

If you live someone else's dream, it will quickly become your nightmare.

APRIL

MAINTAINING HEALTH

Your health is not limited to the physical aspect. It heavily involves your mental state which is the basis for your perspective. Your inner health is expressed outwardly in every area of your life. Healthy thinking yields good actions which lead to a greater likelihood for prosperity. Your productivity and success is based on the health of all of your resources.

APRIL 1

HEALTH
A person's mental or physical condition

The natural body is a temple to be maintained for productivity. You can hoard all of the riches and possessions the world can offer but without good health, you cannot thoroughly enjoy those items. Do not engage in risky actions that can bring severe harm to you. The strongest body needs to be treated delicately and protected. Longevity has its place in the realm of successful people.

How do you manage your most prized possession?

APRIL 2

CURE
Something that corrects or relieves a harmful or disturbing situation

In natural law, for every action there is an equal and opposite reaction. By this logic, every ailment by law has a cure. Throughout history, many sicknesses appeared then were eliminated. The diligence of physicians and researchers saved and improved the lives of numerous people affected by illnesses and conditions. Illnesses will become more threatening, so our tools must also evolve to save humanity.

For every problem and circumstance, there is a definite solution.

APRIL 3

DEATH
The end of an existing entity

Death is not the worst thing to happen to you in life. It is simply the conclusion of a period in time. Death is much more common than most people realize. Our motivation dies when we lose our passion. If we give up on tasks due to the illusion of fear, we will allow our grand ideas to die. Words of discouragement also kill one's creative intent. We hold the power to inspire life and death into situations. The more positivity we speak into life, the better quality of life we will experience.

Death in all forms is an opportunity for renewal and rejuvenation.

APRIL 4

ABSTAIN
To refrain from something by one's own choice

Do you face situations that drain your energy or people in your life who literally waste your time? Do you engage in activities that are not utilizing your talents? If the answer is yes to either of these questions, then it is time to push all of the current busy work to the side. You must redirect your resources so you build productive habits. Get rid of all the things that do not give you the results you are working so hard to reach.

Some things must be removed today as you progress toward a better tomorrow.

APRIL 5

CLEANLINESS
The habit of keeping free of superficial imperfections

In the pursuit of a healthy lifestyle, your actions are the determining factors for success. The way we go about our daily functions must be purposeful and just. Be sure to deceive no one for the sake of getting what you want. People are much more willing to help you along the path when you are open and honest with them. Strive to conduct your actions decently and with order.

Do not expect a helping hand if yours are dirty.

APRIL 6

DANGER
The possibility of suffering harm or injury

Avoid dangerous situations at all costs. Many people are caught in the midst of harm to either themselves or others. Accidents can happen, but we must do our best to minimize these instances. Do not spend time with those who make dangerous choices. If you appear to be in an unsafe position, then leave quickly. We usually can feel something is just not right when we are in the situation.

A warning always comes before destruction.

APRIL 7

QUARANTINE

A state, period, or place of isolation in which people or animals exposed to infectious or contagious disease are placed

In the moments when we lose our way, being alone is a good idea. We must separate ourselves from all outside influences. The most productive way to use this time is reflect on our actions to diagnose the problem. We all fall short and suffer lapses in confidence and judgment. This time alone will give us the opportunity to correct the issues and move forward with a renewed, focused energy.

Weeds will threaten the entire harvest if they are not removed.

APRIL 8

BRUTALITY

The trait of extreme cruelty

To fight over issues never solves any problems – new ones are created. Some people in society think the quicker you are to fight, you are more respected. They are the completely wrong. The lack of control actually shows how much you value and depend on the approval of others. Know the truth for yourself and do not be concerned about what negative comments someone might say. Do not allow another's words to drive you to violence. If people are bold enough to put their hands on you in a violent manner, you then must exercise the right to defend yourself.

Senseless violence is the visual evidence of self-pity.

APRIL 9

SYMPATHY
Feelings of pity and sorrow for someone else's misfortune

The more people you encounter, you will learn of their struggles and disappointing circumstances. People will trust you enough to tell you about their situations but do not relish in the negativity of the moment. Speak prosperity and encouragement into their lives. Give them something positive to use so when good times return, they can remember your contribution to their endurance through the storm.

Giving assistance will benefit those in need much more than giving sympathy.

APRIL 10

SPIRITUALITY
Aspects of life and human experience, which go beyond a purely materialist view of the world

At this point, there are over seven billion people here on Earth. We each look unique and experience a variety of cultural norms. Despite our differences, we share essential elements of life. We all want the best out of ourselves. We desire physical and financial security. We hope tomorrow will be better than today. We all share the same responsibility to leave our world much better than before we arrived.

There are no useless threads woven into the fabric of humanity.

APRIL 11

REPAIR
The action of fixing or mending something

Recognize when situations are not going as expected or tools are not working properly. Lack of any kind will continue to give undesirable results if left uncorrected. A broken element must be fixed as soon as possible so the damage is minimal. In the end, you will save much time and valuable resources.

Do not waste time arguing who will plug the hole in a sinking boat.

APRIL 12

SENSITIVITY
Quality or state of being susceptible to stimulation

Being overly sensitive makes one fickle. The lack of sensitivity makes a person mechanical and lacking intensity. One can interact directly and passionately with the rest of the world when there is a good balance in place. The person will also be able to interact with others regardless of where they are on the emotional spectrum. The better your understanding is of others, the more people you can positively influence.

Understand the feelings of the people to encourage them properly.

APRIL 13

SLEEP

A condition of body and mind in which
the nervous system is inactive

There will be much work to do in order for you to achieve your goals. You must do your best to minimize distractions. Next to hunger, the most common distraction is sleepiness. If you get about seven – eight hours of sleep, you are right on track with the average needed for your body. In addition, sleep has two important benefits. First, this time is used to heal and regenerate the body. Second, your brain solidifies the day's learning. Studies show that your best ideas occur as you are going into and out of sleep. Alpha brain wave patterns are the most active in these moments. Your thoughts even gain power while you sleep.

You must rest well in order to perform well.

APRIL 14

CORRUPTION

Dishonest or fraudulent conduct by those in power,
typically involving bribery.

Scandals are commonly reported these days. Such topics include politics, professional sports and even our favorite retailers. Somewhere along the way, a few people lost sight of their purpose. They allowed the power of dollar signs to cloud their judgment and started to contradict their values. Do not be one of these people. When you become successful, remember you possess a responsibility to yourself, to those around you and to those coming after you.

Do not allow greed of money, fame or pride to
corrupt that which is good.

APRIL 15

LAUGHTER
An expression or appearance of merriment or amusement

Life will introduce many funny and ridiculous events. Some of the situations and allow us to laugh at others, but the majority of them make us laugh at ourselves. Laughter is good for us. It lightens the mood of the tense room and even may be the positive turning point in someone's exhausting week. For some people, sharing a good laugh from a humorous story might be the only bright spot of their day.

Laughter is the best stress reliever and can be enjoyed anywhere.

APRIL 16

REST
To cease work or movement in order to relax,
refresh oneself, or recover strength

Rest is different from actually being asleep. You are fully awake but the key is not only to relax your body but also to ease the tension of your mind. People will often complain that they do they cannot sleep well because they could not turn off their busy mind. To do this, they must create a routine to help them to wind down. Take a warm shower or bath and note the relaxing effects. Reading the book is another common remedy. Find out what works for you and be consistent in how you unwind.

Turn off your ambitious mind when the day's work is completed.

APRIL 17

MORALITY
Principles concerning the distinction between
right and wrong or good and bad behavior

To improve the mental health of the world, we must improve the individuals who comprise every nation. The cornerstone of this task is for all of us to embrace a common idea of what is right and what is wrong. There will be some variance depending on the topics discussed. The fundamental ideas of peace, safety and charity, however, are grounded within all people, not just a small subsection of the population.

We are all responsible for the treatment of our neighbors.

APRIL 18

CLEANSE
To rid of something seen as unpleasant, unwanted, or defiling

Those items not periodically cleaned will make the user vulnerable to sickness and disease. We see this situation occur with food handling and with products that are a normal part of our lives. Refreshment comes from cleaning up these items or areas, but the people need the same treatment. Some of these people introduce the sickness of doubt and the disease of negativity into our lives. You must recognize this and cleanse yourself of these toxic relationships so you can spend more time on productive tasks.

Whatever does not make you better will waste your resources.

APRIL 19

BALANCE
Mental steadiness or emotional stability

Too much of anything is detrimental to you. To possess too much of a bad thing is obvious, but too much of the good thing also is bad for you. You must learn how to balance so the negative affects of extremes do not takeover. For example if you never leave your home, your social skills did not develop. On the other hand, if believe you must always be around people, you will determine all of your value according to other people's standards. Both of these instances restrict the fulfillment of your potential. Simply put, the wise operate with balance as their guide because it gives consistency.

Maintain a balance in all aspects of your life to create the peace you desire.

APRIL 20

AWARENESS
To obtain knowledge or perception of

Awareness has a couple of benefits that most people overlook. First, when you pay close attention, you can quickly notice if you are in an environment that has become dangerous. Self-preservation is the most important aspect of life. Secondly, you are able to see opportunities develop right before you. You may notice someone who could be an integral part of your success plan and be at the right place at the right time for a networking opportunity. A high level of awareness has beneficial results.

Everywhere you go, be aware of your surroundings.

APRIL 21

EMOTIONS
Any of the particular feelings that characterize such a state of mind

Avoid conducting yourself based on your feelings. The decision-making process becomes flawed when someone has reached a point of the anger, fear or sadness. When under the illusion of pressure, it becomes very easy to make a hasty choice just to make the anguish go away. People become vulnerable if they reach this emotional level. Take a moment to think things through and remember this too shall pass.

Control your emotions so you can make clear-headed decisions.

APRIL 22

IMPROVEMENT
A change or addition for the better

Self-improvement is one of the best investments you can make. Each day, we are charged with task to become better than we were yesterday. To do this, we must maximize every moment available to increase opportunities for overall success. Hard work and dedication help to sharpen the skills required to advance to the next level of performance. We must meet the right people, learn the valuable information and do all of the things necessary to move forward.

The distance between where you are and where you want to be equals the amount of improvement you make.

APRIL 23

BREATHE
To inhale and exhale air

You may encounter some stressful moments while working. Some people will begin to fall under the illusion of pressure, which can occur among peers and managers. Take the time during such moments to remind everyone involved of the original reason they are here. Restore the purpose within people and the strategy for success will help to settle them down to return them to the express track of productivity.

When there is tension, regroup on common ground.

APRIL 24

POLLUTION
The introduction of harmful substances or
products into the environment

Be careful of what you put into your body. Unnatural items often are associated directly with health risks. This ranges from processed foods to prescription drugs. Man-made substances often cause the body to react with adverse side effects which sometimes can be lethal depending on circumstances. Natural remedies prove to be much more beneficial to the body rather than the synthetic alternative.

Unnatural things act as pollutants to the body.

APRIL 25

GROWTH
The act or process of developing

Any time used for growth is for your development and the cultivation of others. As we walk along our determined path, we are able to encourage many people a long way. A majority of the time, we do not even need to say a word in order to relay the message. The internal struggles and external challenges are all important pieces used to inform others that they too can overcome adversity. Your strength during the process will precede you.

Never underestimate the power of your journey.

APRIL 26

GENETICS
The science of passing traits from an organism to its offspring

If a son or daughter looks at the triumphs or disappointments of their parents, is it certain that those experiences will happen to children? No, this is absolutely false. The conditions endured may be similar, but each child has the opportunity to change the pace of their lives. Life is flexible. There is no such thing as being locked into a doomed existence.

A condition before you is not destined to happen to you.

APRIL 27

EXERCISE
Bodily or mental exertion, especially for the sake
of training or improvement of health

If the mind is the driving force to visualize all aspirations, the body is the primary tool used to accomplish them. Physical exertion also regulates hormone and physiological balances to relieve various stresses. In many cases of illness, exercise sure as many elements when the companied by a healthy diet. The more active you are now, the more active you can be as you mature.

Condition your body just as you would condition your mind.

APRIL 28

ADDICTION
The object of a physiological or psychological dependency

Many of us struggle with a variety of addictions. These addictions can include substance abuse, lying and even high consumption of junk food. We must find the strength to know that we do not "need" the object of our addiction – it needs us. Without us, it has no life or purpose. Without us, it has no commanding force. What positive action or idea can we substitute in its place? The old addictions will be transformed into our new hobbies when we learn to consistently make such an exchange.

*When you decide you have had enough,
your addictions will lose the power you gave it.*

APRIL 29

ENERGY
*The strength & vitality required to sustain
a physical or mental activity*

Energy is a tangible entity. After walking into a crowded room, observe those who add to the fun and excitement compared to those who drain others with their negativity. People naturally thrive off each other because energy naturally flows from one source to another. Fill your cup of enthusiasm and allow it to overflow so others can receive the surplus.

Your positive energy will inspire people to move mountains.

APRIL 30

DEPRESSION
*A condition of mental disturbance, accompanied by feelings
of hopelessness, inadequacy and lack of energy*

Depression is a very serious and life-threatening condition that is treatable and avoidable. We all experience varying degrees of it throughout life, yet it has a common remedy. The primary cause of depression is the illusion of fear, which is centered on what horrible event "could" happen. There is no such thing as fear. Just because things may not go as a planned, there is no need to be afraid. You must first believe that things will get better than the current circumstances then work toward making these changes happen. With time and focused passion, depression is replaced by triumph.

*The cure for depression resides in your goals and
your ability to accept life's results.*

MASTERING YOUR CONNECTIONS

The next stage of peace highlights all of the people connected to you. Your family, friends and associates serve as catalysts for increasing the opportunities for your success. The relationships that you foster, whether long-term or short-term, will create challenges that you must overcome. But through these connections of people, you will discover great value in them because they serve to sharpen your ability to resolve conflicts.

MAY

FAMILY TIES

The family structure plays a vital role in personal development. It is the primary source of interactions that teaches us how to govern ourselves. We also are exposed to the concepts of selflessness and cooperation. The fundamentals of how we form personal relationships are established within the family. All families encounter challenging times, but in such moments, the unit will prevail when it operates within the confines of forgiveness, accountability and truth.

MAY 1

HONESTY
The quality or condition of being truthful

Honesty is the expression of one's personal truth. You must tell the truth despite any consequences and avoid the stress of remembering lies. Honest expression is the way to respect yourself and gain respect from others. It establishes a base of trust, which is essential in all relationships. The value of your word is directly linked to how honorable you are.

Honesty is the foundation of all fruitful relationships.

MAY 2

FATHERS
The male parental unit of a family

The role of the father is to manage the progression of the home. A father must exemplify strong work ethics and discipline so everyone else in the home learns the importance of these skills. Effective fathers are "big picture" thinkers. He is a major decision maker and knows the value of gathering information from his spouse's perspective. Much responsibility falls on a father's shoulders because the quality of his decisions will affect all of the other family members. The father who generally inspires his family toward greatness will leave a legacy for his children's grandchildren.

A good father lays the groundwork for the family's path.

MAY 3

HOME
The place where one lives

A house is nothing more than a structure used to provide shelter for its inhabitants. In order for any dwelling to become a home, the environment and must be warm and loving. If there is tension or strife, the climate can become uncomfortable and the negative energy is easily recognized by others. A home's positive energy is not only beneficial to the residents. As people interact, positive energy can influence other households and leave fruitful and lasting impressions.

Home is wherever the heart resides with peace.

MAY 4

LOYALTY
Faithfulness to commitments or obligations

The key to loyalty is to finding and fighting for a common cause. We sometimes assume the loyalty of close friends and family would be automatic but this not always the case. Their eyes may not be opened to the common cause, but it is their right to choose. Be sure to place your loyalty the right situations. If you find a noble cause and you have the resources available to you, then participate. You often uncover significant benefits because of your dedication.

The loyalty you exhibit can reap surprising rewards.

MAY 5

APPRECIATION
The recognition & gratitude of the qualities of someone or something

An important lesson the family teaches is to be thankful for what you possess. Other than your spouse, you cannot choose your relatives. The family is a small reflection of the world, so you may encounter members that have views and personalities different from you. The family is the first instance where you are encouraged to accept people for who they are and give support unconditionally. Despite the differences of opinion or even misunderstandings, the role of each family member is to teach and hold each other accountable for the strengthening of the family name.

Be thankful for the people and circumstances that sum up your life.

MAY 6

INDEPENDENCE
Freedom from the control, influence or aid of others

The road to independence is often a tedious one. As children, those close to us may have seen us in need and instantly provide solutions. This a loving gesture does not develop the skills to be self-sufficient. A more beneficial alternative is for the child to make multiple attempts at the task. Afterwards, the adult can teach the correct procedure so the child can perform the task in successful manner without assistance. Through the failed attempts, the child gains context for the task, which makes it much easier to learn to proper procedures.

Strive to become self-sufficient and teach others to do the same.

MAY 7

GUIDANCE
Advice or information aimed at resolving a problem or difficulty

Every stable and successful family includes a few members who give guidance to help the next generation. Such mentors help to teach what they have learned so the other members can reach their goals. Look within your family to discover the wise relatives to ask for advice. Your confidence increases when you know someone is there to walk you through the procedures. Those who mastered the skills needed to succeed profess that preparation is determined by hard work. Work is nothing more than a series of procedures.

*Watch a previous champion
to learn how to win.*

MAY 8

PREJUDICE
Preconceived opinion not based on reason or experience.

Prejudice has been proven to be learned ignorance throughout history. People have been ridiculed because of being left handed, short in height, having small eyes and even walking slowly. All of them have had negative connotations attached to them because someone was too lazy to get to know them personally. Instead of taking the time to invest in learning about them they assume all people are the same based on the scope of their limited experience. The person prejudging actually hinders their own progress because opportunities are present within all people, not just a select few.

*The person you show prejudice toward could be
the one who positively changes your life.*

MAY 9

GENEROSITY
The willingness and liberality in giving away one's possessions

Humanity is tribal in nature. The most prosperous societies build their philosophy built around a single idea – sharing. As each person works to store ample resources, any excess can be shared by the rest of the people. There is an automatic tendency for us to see those in need and help them as much as we can. We must be sure to give our resources to others, however do not cause injury to ourselves. As long as those resources are truly the extra portion, we all will be just fine.

People with the spirit of generosity never go without.

MAY 10

PARENTING
The care and upbringing of a child

There is no ultimate guidebook for parenting, but there are a few ideas to will provide a solid foundation. 1) Remember, you are the parent, not your child's friend. Children will not respect the adults who do not respect their own parental position. 2) Set reasonable standards and hold everyone accountable. Without discipline, there is chaos. 3) Do not rush to your children's side <u>every</u> time you think they need you. If the children are not bleeding, dying or on fire, they will be all right. Lastly, allow them to find and experience failure because this is where determination and success live.

Teach the children that they can achieve all things and know that you still can, too.

MAY 11

ELDERS
A person of greater age than someone specified

Experience is an extremely valuable commodity no matter what age you are. Those older than you often have valuable knowledge for you to use. For example, the technology of the telephone evolved into how we communicate with the Internet today. We must learn from our Elders and process the information to create advanced ideas. More importantly, this must be applied to life. There is nothing new at all. Speak to those who are insightful on how to live a balanced, productive life. This will give you wisdom to handle all the events you encounter positively. You then can pass on your wisdom when you eventually become the elder.

Listening to those more experienced than you can save you much time and energy.

MAY 12

TACT
The skill of dealing with difficult or delicate situations

We may not always agree on all issues when communicating with loved ones. Some situations can lead to full blown arguments. We must remember "how" to communicate with each other to avoid problems moving forward. In all sensitive conversations, we must remember to show respect and give our perspective with love. Truth is better received when invoked in peace and hand delivered without fumbling or sugar coating. The responsibility resides with the recipients to use the information you have given them to improve their lives.

You can say anything on your mind when you sincerely say it with love.

MAY 13

SHARE
To allow someone to use or enjoy something the one's possesses

Everyone has an area of skills and a field of expertise which can be useful for others. To find your area, consider the things that you are passionate about or something that you can do better than most people. Life demands us to share our knowledge with others in order to reach a prosperous existence. Give your time, talents or words of encouragement so we can pass along the information to generations to come.

You live a more fulfilling life when you share your talents with the world

MAY 14

RESOLUTION
The settling of a problem

Within family matters, we often make excuses for the shortcomings of those we love, which does more harm to them than good. Resolve situations swiftly when actions need to be corrected. Without correction, those who did wrong may start to believe their actions are acceptable when they clearly are not. Unresolved issues only create a natural bitterness and tension amongst the members of the family.

Always bring resolution to a situation so it does not grow into a much larger problem.

MAY 15

ATTENTION
To regard someone or something as interesting or important

All members of the family are valuable. In each of our lives, the struggles of making a living can reduce our free time so much that we forget to contact our families. We must do our best to keep open lines of communication. From small children all the way up to the older members of the family, we must make a valiant effort to reach out to let each other know they are important. Life will throw countless obstacles our way, but we can help each other through those turbulent times so we can enjoy our triumphs together.

Each seed planted holds the power of beauty and purpose.

MAY 16

MOTHERS
The female parental unit of a family

The mother's irreplaceable role begins well before the child arrives. She must maintain her body so that the child develops well. The good mother helps to create a positive environment for the child to grow in stature and intellect. The mother's sacrifice and dedication is unlike any other. She wants the best the world can offer for her child and instills qualities within him or her to become a productive member of society.

***A good mother is the heartbeat of the home
and the center of the family.***

MAY 17

DIVISION
The action or process of separating something into parts

Division is one of the worst conditions experienced within the family. Avoid such devastation at all costs. Division is a byproduct of disrespect, mistrust and lack of understanding. The family, under such circumstances, does not operate efficiently as the source for education and assistance. Our respectable differences of opinion should never inspire hatred or disdain for each other. Remember to find common ground for both parties to agree upon and work together toward a solution when faced with such tough times.

Division is the biggest obstacle in a family's progress.

MAY 18

TREASURE
A quantity of precious metals, gems, or other valuable objects

What I think of my sister and brothers, I remember a few, distinct experiences. I remember my sister taking time to teach me advanced mathematics when I was seven years old and just because I wanted to match her intelligence. I remember my brothers teaching me how to play sports, musical instruments and even making egg sandwiches for me because I was too young to cook. My most valued possessions are these kinds of treasured family moments. When life gets tough, these are the memories that I use to put a smile of my face and remember that everything will be OK.

A family's greatest assets are to have memorable life experiences and harmony amongst its members.

MAY 19

HABITS
A regular tendency or practice difficult to give up

We are taught to be good growing up. We often still experimented with many things, but we remembered to hold on to the good habits that produced the desired results. The occasional recklessness of our youth evolves into fruitful actions and can teach others how to be successful. To speak the truth and follow-through on your promises are essential habits for life. In the working environment, finish your work before deadlines to leave room for revision and resolve conflicts respectfully. These may seem basic, but few people adhere to these good habits.

Your greatest work of art is shaped by the blueprint of your smallest habits.

MAY 20

SUPPORT
To maintain a person, family, establishment or institution by supplying the things necessary for its existence

We understand the importance of helping those in need. Another area we must consider is our role as a piece of a support system. As people around us actively pursue their goals, we must remind them that they can be successful by continuing on their chosen course of action. Often, those working toward goals are forgotten because everyone else believes the success will come easily for them. These people, however, need your kind words and pats on the back the most to energize them all the way to the finish line.

Support from our family breathes life into our purpose.

MAY 21

IMPOSTERS

A person who deceives others by assuming a false identity

Unfortunately, just because someone is a part of your family, that does not mean that he or she is here to benefit you. Some of the main people who you believe should have your best interests in mind, may not. These people may be difficult to recognize because when you interact with them, there is a pleasant exchange. If you interact with people who always want something from you, then they are sponging off you. There is nothing at all wrong with saying no and going on about your business. It does not mean that you do not love them. You recognize the fact that if they are not adding any value to you, then they are reducing your value by draining your resources.

People's actions will always tell you more than their words.

MAY 22

ACCEPTANCE

The act of taking or receiving something offered

For some people, no matter how much you do for them, they still may not choose to do the right things. They may continue to complain about their situation without working to improve the circumstances. They may even blame everyone else for the pitfalls of their lives without taking responsibility for their actions. People mature at their own pace no matter how desperate you are to help them.

Learn to accept situations when they are beyond your control.

MAY 23

RELIANCE
To depend on or trust in someone or something

We are all busy with meeting the demands of life. For this reason, we should be able to reach out to our families for what we may need. One would think this is the most important part but is not. If you are in need and another family member does not or cannot help you, does that mean he or she does not love you? Of course not. The most important aspect is the willingness for the person to help you. This is the essential mentality of a family – an unyielding willingness to help each other.

As each person's duty is fulfilled, the group will prosper.

MAY 24

AMBITION
A strong desire to do or to achieve something

Ambition is very similar to water – too much and too little can be bad for you. The overly ambitious experience the headaches of having too much to do and no time to do it. The lack of ambition results in laziness and wasted resources. Avoid these extremes and work to maintain a balance of ambition. Make time to work on your various projects for a predetermined amount of time, and then give yourself sufficient time for a rest and relaxation period. Follow this process to better organize your efforts.

Kindle the fire of your loved one's noble goals.

MAY 25

POISE
The state of balance and stability in a person

We often find ourselves under time constraints and various performance anxieties. Sometimes we want to reach our goals so badly, that we lose our focus. During such intense moments, we must remember that we can only tackle one obstacle at a time. If there is an abundance of work to be completed, ask for help and delegate the tasks. By doing this, you can refocus on the essential parts of the project and work more efficiently toward the deadline.

The cool & calm often make better choices in the midst of chaos.

MAY 26

CONSEQUENSES
A result or effect of an action or condition

If you touch a hot stove, you may be burned. This idea applies to everyone and is a great example of consequences. Our actions dictate what type of consequence we receive. We increase the likelihood to receive rewards if we perform good actions. On the contrary, if our actions are bad or negative, we are bound to receive some form of punishment. This is one of nature's most basic laws – we will reap what we sow. With this in mind, we must be fully aware of our actions and sow positivity to ensure the good energy will come back to us.

The path of least resistance is often paved with regret.

MAY 27

DINNER
The main meal of the day eaten in the evening

Food naturally unites people. Historically, families would discuss the events of the day over a meal, but recently we have gotten away from the practice. Our technology has consumed our attention to replace the valuable conversations we would have with loved ones. We must work this practice back into our daily lives. Dinner is a bonding time for everyone. In addition, these are the moments when you learn the most about the personalities within your family. The family who grows up together can reflect on all of the joyous times when everyone can sit, eat and laugh together.

*To discover your family's vibrant personality,
give them a full plate of food.*

MAY 28

CONTACT
Immediate proximity or association

It is good to keep in contact with your family. Even if it is only to call and see how they are doing, the gesture goes a long way. It leaves a positive feeling with them to know that someone cared enough to reach out to them. Start by contacting one person a day, even if only for a few moments. Maintain close relations with the family in case of an emergency.

Never assume your family knows your intentions.

MAY 29

COACH
A person who instructs a student for a performance

We all have special talents to share with the world in some field. Giving guidance to help others is good but if you have the time and resources, become a coach for someone who is willing to learn your craft. The difference is that coaches spend much more time teaching the pupil the nature of the desired craft. What field have you mastered and who could be seeking the knowledge you possess?

Someone close to you can benefit from your detailed resume.

MAY 30

CHILDREN
A young human being below the age of full physical development

The children are much more than our future; they are our "now". The technological advancements and their determination have empowered our youth to become a multimillionaire CEOs and leaders of philanthropic organizations. With such vast opportunities in front of them, it is our duty to expose them to various fields and instill qualities of strong work ethic within them. We must set the bar high and assist them in every noble way to help them achieve their goals. Most importantly, we must be the example of a kind, focused, successful citizens to inspire them to be the same.

All children are gifts of extraordinary potential.

MAY 31

REPRESENT
To stand for or to symbolize

We each come from unique backgrounds and experience life in various ways. Despite those differences, it is important to note that wherever we may go in life, we represent what we are taught at home. Whether you visit a city, state, or even another country, how you represent yourself is vital to your success. It also directly points back to how you apply the manners, compassion and determination instilled in you long ago. There is no such thing as the perfect home but we all understand right from wrong. When you know better, you should do better.

Do your actions align with your positive "home training"?

JUNE

THE WORLD AROUND YOU

The people that you interact with outside of your family are pivotal to your achievements. As you interact with others, you learn new concepts and procedures that can better yourself. They also can help you to find your place in the world by giving essential feedback on issues that you may overlook. The more that you learn of your surroundings, the quality of your decision-making can improve. Your social circles will dictate the opportunities that will come your way.

JUNE 1

GLOBAL

To be universal and pertaining to the whole world

Every person, no matter what the age, is a valuable contributor to humanity. Our technology now allows us to contact people instantly across the world. Each nation has resources to be used to create industries so the other countries may benefit. The smallest idea can spread to a majority of the world's inhabitants in a matter of moments. Collaborations are not bound by locality. Partners thousands of miles away from each other can conduct business. Which of your ideas can change the world?

At over 7 billion people, we are Earth's most valuable resource.

JUNE 2

TRUST

Firm belief in the reliability or strength of someone or something

Trust is an essential component of interaction. There is no reason at all to converse with a person if you cannot believe the validity of his or her statements. You also must be careful of who you trust. Does it make sense to entrust someone whose word is inconsistent? Is it logical to trust someone who lies to you? To hold this expectation of others, we must exhibit these qualities as well. Be truthful in speech despite what the masses accept. Let your actions reflect the truth that you believe so you develop consistency. The more consistent you are with your words and actions the more people will be able to rely on you.

For others to have confidence in you, you must be trustworthy.

JUNE 3

ENVIRONMENT
The surroundings or conditions in which one lives or operates

We commonly think of natural surroundings and endangered species of animal world when the environment is mentioned. We must be wise use our natural resources and reduce the impact of our carbon footprints, yet, are you treating your personal environment the same? Plants need sunlight, soil and water to fulfill its purposes of providing oxygen and beauty to the world. What do you need to fulfill your purposes? Who shines inspiration into your life? What knowledge gives you a sturdy foundation from which to grow? What circumstances shower your determination? Use these answers to prune your personal environment for successful development.

Create the environment that supports your ambitions.

JUNE 4

HOSPITALITY
The friendly and generous reception and entertainment of guests

We must live together harmoniously, so it is good to host events to build stronger bonds with your guests. These types of functions are valuable opportunities for exchanges of ideas and life experiences. The perspective from others allows you to further cultivate your ideas and inspire others to expand their thinking as well. Often great business ideas are created and nourished by meeting up with others over a meal. By doing this on a consistent basis, for you can enhance the lives of everyone involved.

Your hospitality will grant you favor with all of your guests.

JUNE 5

VENGEANCE

Punishment inflicted or retribution exacted for an injury or wrong.

Moments will arise where you feel you have been wronged. Nothing productive occurs when you choose to do evil to those who do evil to you. People who knowingly do wrong toward others are creating doom for themselves. The same negative energy that they are putting out will return to them. How and when justice is served is not your concern. Laws and enforcement entities are present to encourage peaceful resolutions when seeking justice.

Seek justice by the proper means – never by your own rules.

JUNE 6

TEMPERANCE

Self-restraint or moderation of thought and action

The illusion of fear can cause people to feel pressure and push them to their boiling point. Give encouraging words to help relieve some of the pressure or anxiety. In other cases, you may witness them lose control of themselves and display uncontrollable sadness and hostile outbursts of anger. We are all accountable for our reactions and possess the complete ability to control our actions. You, however, are not responsible for one other person does. You are only responsible for ensuring your conduct is good and sound.

Watching other fireworks does not give you the right to explode.

JUNE 7

COMMUNICATION
The imparting or exchanging of information

Centuries ago, sending a message to someone overseas would take 4 to 5 months. A few years ago, sending the message by mail would have taken a couple of weeks. With today's technology, to communicate with someone overseas takes only a few seconds. We access extraordinary channels for communication yet the messages are filled with idle talk. We stand on huge platforms to speak to the world but of messages lack depth of meaning and purpose. Your voice matters. It can be used inspire, teach and heal the world. The thoughtful messages you deliver will change the course of history.

Never underestimate the power of your words.

JUNE 8

SOCIETY
The community of people living in a particular region
and having shared customs, laws, and organizations

Pay close attention to how society creates its own rules about what is acceptable in what is not. Societies can be on the evolutionary edge of useful information to benefit your life however, it may profess ideas and beliefs that contradict your own. For this reason, you must be aware of what is happening in society without being bound to it. Some people will follow others regardless of the issue, but as long as you utilize your ability to think independently, you will become a worthy trendsetter instead of a mindless follower.

*Be quick to notice the movements of
society, but slow to follow them.*

JUNE 9

PATRIOTISM
Love of country and willingness to sacrifice for it

Nothing is wrong with having pride for one's national origin. Your heritage is to be celebrated. The pride one possesses, however, should not derive from the disdain for another nation. The degrading of another's origin does not enrich your own. Your value decreases due to your lack of understanding. Know who you are and do not degrade other people. Take the time to learn about their heritage and assist them when needed. We cannot allow the territorial borders to restrict the fair treatment of others.

Never allow patriotism to resemble discrimination.

JUNE 10

BOUNDARIES
A dividing line marking the limits of an area

Boundaries help to set the expectation for what is to come. At the basic level, territorial boundaries serve to outline who was responsible for a certain area. This applies directly to how we interact with each other. When given tasks, we must communicate well with each other so we do not invade another's area of responsibility. As we pursue goals and upward mobility of employment, avoid stepping on toes to get what you want.

Know your role and be careful not to overstep your boundaries.

JUNE 11

MEDIOCRITY
Of only ordinary or barely adequate quality

In school, some people are satisfied with the minimal passing grade. To do the very best you can and barely pass is noble. However, if you only give just enough effort to reach the minimum, then you are doing yourself of real disservice. No matter how challenging the task, you should always strive for the maximum. This applies not only with school but also in how we should live our lives. To be mediocre, you need no special skills or knowledge. You should always think more of yourself and work hard to stand out from the crowd to avoid being content with living an average, cookie-cutter life.

Mediocrity is a destination that one should never reach.

JUNE 12

AGREE
To be of the same opinion about something

Machines work efficiently and tasks are accomplished when all of the gears are working together. Each gear has its own duty but still is essential to the whole. People operate in a similar fashion. The most productive groups will begin with the same idea in mind – the reason inspiring them to participate. The work must then be distributed so when everyone has completed the tasks, the overall job is done. Power lives in agreement. The communal force becomes much stronger when people share the same understanding for the mission.

Prosperity never exists where discord resides.

JUNE 13

COMPROMISE
To settle a dispute by mutual concession

In business and in life, no one will agree with you on everything. We all have our own values, backgrounds and perspectives to shape our decision-making standards. To work together toward a compromise allows us to share a mutually beneficial vision. While negotiating terms, each party involved must sacrifice something to create the win-win situation needed for everyone to walk away with more than they initially had.

Even if we both lose a little today, we can gain a lot tomorrow.

JUNE 14

COMPANY
Those who you associate with

The people who we spend the most time with are all reflections of ourselves in some way. This common trait could be the love of sports, working in similar fields or even having children of the same age. Always seek opportunities to spend time with people who match well with your good qualities and positive situations. Those will be the same people to push you to improve your current self.

The company that you keep speaks volumes about you.

JUNE 15

FAIRNESS
Free from bias or injustice

Fairness is natural to humanity when at its best. We strive to live in communities where harmony and justice are abundant. Some individuals will unjustly accuse us or treat us without fairness. These people are either allowing greed to overcome them or they have not yet reached full development to understand how to operate within productive societies. Where there is fairness, you can establish expectations. You can set goals in an efficient manner when there are measurable expectations. We cannot accept instances of unfairness as a standard of living. We are the commanders of our lives. We hold the power to create a world that bends as we see fit for ourselves and future generations.

In all of your dealings with people, be fair and honest.

JUNE 16

RESTRAINT
The action of keeping someone or something under control

We encounter situations that will seem to ignite our emotions. We may feel enraged from a wrongdoing toward us or overwhelmed from the sadness of coping with a loss. Some opportunities will be presented to advance ourselves but they may contradict our values and beliefs. We must resist such urges. Although we may have the ability and opportunity to do something that does not mean we should. We will be held accountable for our actions even if provoked by emotions or opportunities for selfish gain.

Controlling yourself takes only a moment, not a lifetime.

JUNE 17

ICONS

A person or thing highly regarded as a symbol of a
belief, nation, community, or cultural movement

In a world of constant advertising and brand recognition campaigns we are overwhelmed with people telling us what we should think about other people. The public will place certain people on a pedestal and treat them better just because they may be famous. These days, to be regarded as an icon for a group of people, no skills or in the special talents are required. These so-called icons are displayed as the epitome of that which we all should aspire. However, this is just another type of illusion aimed to control your life. Do not buy into empty heroes.

A higher level of popularity does not increase one's character.

JUNE 18

MANIPULATION

To exert shrewd or devious influence for one's own advantage

Manipulation and guidance may seem similar. There is one person giving a recommendation while another executes this recommendation. If this is questioned, examine who receives the benefit of the action or task of being completed. If the person giving the recommendation also receives the benefit, then it is a possibility that they performed an act of manipulation. If the person executing the advice receives the benefit, then guidance has occurred. It is good to consider this is so the manipulation is recognized and time is not wasted.

*The difference between manipulation and guidance
is defined by who benefits the most.*

JUNE 19

CHARISMA
Compelling attractiveness or charm to can inspire devotion in others

People who exhibit charisma are difficult to miss. Strong belief in an idea generates an uncontrollable energy within you. Soon, you will want to share the idea with others so they can experience the same joy, strength or knowledge that invigorates you. Positive energy is infectious. It is a powerful tool to use when seeking to inform people or move them progressively.

The intensity of your enthusiasm can make a believer of anyone.

JUNE 20

FAD
A temporary fashion or manner of conduct followed by a group

A huge amount of energy and effort is placed upon consumers. Marketing and advertising campaigns are all geared toward making the public think in a specific way about various products and services. The general public sways easily based on what products or services are deemed popular. Yet, does an overpriced piece of clothing withhold more value just because more people wear it. The answer is a resounding no. Opinions will change based on the newest fashion craze. Do not be influenced by such novelty.

Possessing good quality is much more rewarding than having that which is popular.

JUNE 21

FRIENDSHIP

Interpersonal relationships considered to be closer than association

"Friend" is one of the most misused words in society. Only those who have proven themselves worthy of the title should be called friends. One should never call another a friend for the sake of being nice. To be a friend is a responsibility. A friend expects the best of others by giving constructive criticism and leading others away from negative situations. A friend is willing to help you when needed yet will tell you when you are wrong. How many people do you know actually meet these qualifications of a real friend? More importantly, do you meet this standard?

Friendship is a responsibility, not a right.

JUNE 22

RANK

A position in the hierarchy of an organization

There is no need to contact everyone in a crowded room in hopes to pursue your goal. It only takes one person. One key decision-maker can provide an opportunity to advance and change the course of your life. The people who possess the power to execute tasks will always be within an organizational hierarchy. Consult with the people on the lower areas of the totem pole and ask them to point out who holds the ultimate power of the decision.

Speak directly to the decision-makers to get tasks completed.

JUNE 23

TOLERATION
A fair and permissive attitude toward opinions
and practices different from one's own

The general public is full of a variety of concepts and perspectives. Occasionally, personalities will have difficulty interacting with each other. Some people's belief systems can be so detached that they are closed-minded to a different way of viewing ideas. The best feature of humanity is not how unique we are, but our acceptance of the good traits we introduce to the world. We will accomplish much more when we unify than what we could when divided.

*I may disagree with your methods, but I
respect the roots of your position.*

JUNE 24

ADVANTAGE
A condition or circumstance putting one in a favorable position

With the population over seven billion and counting, competition is intense for resources and opportunities to get what you desire. Many people who share the same aspirations as you, so how can you increase your odds of success? Find qualities and circumstances to set you apart from the rest of the crowd. These may include procedures that allow you to perform tasks faster and with better quality than others. Knowing the right partners who own resources to improve your products also is a unique way to distinguish yourself. The more often such advantages are attained, the probability of your success increases dramatically.

*Seek every decent advantage to separate
yourself from the competition.*

JUNE 25

BENEVOLENCE
The desire to do good to others

To be a productive member within a community, one must possess a spirit of benevolence. We naturally give and receive help before we learned to walk and speak. A region whose inhabitants possess this ideal can grow to be holistically sound and inspire the country. Such a country can lead by example to show the world how caring and goodness is fundamental to the human experience. We imitate the actions before us. If we can manage to display more sincere charitable instances, the rest of the world will follow suit accordingly.

Do everything within your power to help people in their moment of need because your time is coming soon.

JUNE 26

ABUSE
To treat in a harmful, injurious, or offensive way

Some people who find the illusion of their strength in abusing others. These culprits, at times, will be the closest people to us. Talk to someone who you trust for advice if you are being physically abused. For those who might be verbally abused, remember that words only retain is much power as you give them. Always consider the source. Abusers lack self-esteem, so to compensate they berate others. Abuse is never a byproduct of love, it is the lack thereof.

Neither give nor accept any form of abuse.

JUNE 27

AFFILIATION
To be associated with a person or organization

Whether service or socially oriented, organizations provide a virtuous platform to join people within a common cause. The service type of organization provides the means of giving resources of time or funds to those in need for the betterment of the community. Social groups, however, usually include members linked by common bond of shared ideas such a sports, food, etc. The time spent within organizations serves to expand your personal horizon by giving you new ideas and experiences. By expanding your network of contacts, opportunities for can bloom organically from such interactions.

Support organizations that share your ideas and values.

JUNE 28

AUTHENTIC
Of genuine and undisputed origin

Popularity and power are prizes that can cause people to lose all inhibitions. Some people will do anything to attain them. It is extremely important to choose the people in your life wisely. In such cases where these people are relatives, you must use your best judgment as to how long you interact with them. If you take inventory of the people in your life, do all of them want the best for you? Do any of them constantly use you? You can do without these people. Find those who want prosperity for you and hold them close.

Fill your life with authentic people because they will have your best interest in mind.

JUNE 29

RESOURCES
A collection of supply, support, or aid to be used when needed

In order to reach goals, you must have the necessary resources. The key is to gather as many resources as possible so that when the time arrives to execute your plans, everything runs smoothly. Of course, you cannot have everything at your disposal, yet, you may know the people who do. The most prosperous people in the world know networks of others who may access their resources for use. This is an example of the power of networking. Having access to resources is always better than actually possessing them.

The world is full of ample resources when you are brave enough to seek them.

JUNE 30

HUMANITY
The condition of human beings collectively

Humans live a highly communal existence. The nature of human interaction shows that as the few progress, we all progress. If one person has an abundance of resources, there must be a mechanism in place for the benefit of the people. Some may choose to volunteer their time & resources to share with those in need while others establish their own charitable foundations to operate. Issues of world hunger, poverty and violence must be addressed not only by the powerful countries but every nation. If we share our best practices for life, economy and charity, the world will be much improved.

We all are responsible for the advancement of human progress.

JULY

MANAGING RELATIONSHIPS

As long as there are two people interacting, there is always the chance for discord. Whether family or close friends, we will have differences of opinion on certain topics. If we encounter such challenges with people we know, it is guaranteed that we will encounter them with those we do not. The key in such cases is finding common ground. As you value positive relationships, they will add value to you.

JULY 1

RESPECT
The state of being regarded with honor or esteem

The foundation of all relationships is respect. This has a reciprocal quality and benefits all involved. You show respect by valuing the thoughts and contributions of others. The work toward a solution can be done in a cordial fashion when there is a disagreement or difference of opinion. If there is no agreement to be reached, all parties can except the situation and move forward peacefully. The more genuine respect you show others, the more honor will be associated with you.

Respect is only received by those who consistently give it.

JULY 2

COMPASSION
Deep awareness of the suffering coupled with
the desire to relieve the discomfort

The tribal nature of humanity requires us to be compassionate to help each other cope with the unfavorable experiences of life. The hearts of the people will become cold and hard if we do not invest this energy to help others. Bitterness and hatred are the only byproducts that can come from a heart empty of love. Let us treat each other with dignity so we make our elders proud and our children can grow in a disciplined, loving environment.

*The essence of humanity lies in our
compassion toward each other.*

JULY 3

CHARITY
Provision of help or relief to those in need

Acts of charity establish and develop positive relationships. This goes beyond simply giving something to another. Charity is a direct expression of the perfection of humanity. In a well-developed society, the people assist their neighbors by wisely giving their time and resources. This cyclical nature of giving improves the lives of all participants. Wisdom in giving is necessary to ensure that your charitable efforts are not detrimental to your personal situation. In other words, give from your extra resources, not from your needed resources.

Those who are free to give constantly receive.

JULY 4

BATTLE
An encounter between opposing forces

Battles with others, whether inside or outside of the home, drain your sensitivity and energy. In most cases, this even distorts your ability to make sound judgments. The key to winning battles is to minimize the number of those conflicts. All battles must be ended in a swift and direct manner, if needed. Without closure, these moments can become life-draining episodes and leave you losing more than what you could gain in victory.

Battles are created by the absence of comfort and understanding.

JULY 5

CONTEMPT
The state of being despised or dishonored

In life, relationships will encounter ebbs and flows. There will be people who will perpetually disagree with you and harbor contempt toward you no matter what you do. Sometimes, the people who you assist the most will hold the most disdain for you. When you know that you have done no wrong and have not misled them in any way, leave them be. The best thing you can do is to grant them the time to work through their shortcomings and self-medicate. Everyone faces challenges that must be worked through, however some conquer those challenges sooner than others.

I am not responsible for the lies you choose to believe.

JULY 6

COOPERATION
The association of persons or businesses for common benefit

Your efforts are multiplied exponentially when you work with others. How much can you do in the completion of a task? The answer is 100%. To manage tasks by yourself reduces confusion and allows you to make all decisions, however, you must do everything. Now consider if you added three more people to help tackle the same task. You now can delegate if to others. The amount everyone is responsible for now is reduced to 25%. This drastic reduction of effort allows you to focus in on the smaller duties to complete them more efficiently. Such approaches allow for fresh ideas to improve other areas of production or performance.

If you want to achieve quickly, go alone.
If you want lasting success, go together.

JULY 7

MERCY
Leniency toward an offender or adversary

You will encounter people who are physically strong and try to intimidate others by force to get what they want. These misguided individuals believe the appearance of strength is the same as actual strength. This is not true. When you are truly powerful, there is no need to boast or put on a show to exhibit your power. Your strength will emerge as you interact with people. Through the truth that you profess and the fortitude of your actions, your undeniable power will speak for itself.

Power is not expressed by brute force, but in the gentleness of strength.

JULY 8

DECEPTION
A misleading falsehood

In close relationships, the trust of a loved one's word is expected to be high. In some moments, unfortunately, those same people may deceive you in order to get something they want or avoid the possible tarnishing of their name. A good practice is to invest little into what some people say and pay close attention to what they do. People will act in their own best interests more often than not. Follow their actions to discover where the truth resides.

Watch a person's actions to reveal the real intentions.

JULY 9

DATING

An engagement to go out socially with another
person, often out of romantic interest

The dating scene can be one of the most nerve-wracking aspects of seeking a longtime partner, however there are a few ways to minimize the negative experiences. Seek those who make a habit of honesty. A fruitful relationship does not develop if the other person cannot be honest with you. Without trust, you have nothing. Also, do not smother the relationship. Give space and opportunity for blossoming. Rushing often leads to mistakes and misjudged situations. Seek partners who are confident, ambitious and unselfish. All of the great qualities that you seek should already be in your possession.

Some of the most of the wonderful people in the world are meant to be just friends.

JULY 10

KINDNESS

The quality of being warmhearted and humane

The life experience is filled with love and kindness. Without it, life would be hopeless and violent. Humanity was not designed to live under such conditions. We must relate to each other and interact with thoughtfulness and justice. Even in challenging moments when we must correct the actions of others, we can proceed in a caring, yet stern way. The person committing the offense can then understand the situation and remedy their wrongdoing without losing self-respect. Kindness has a liberating quality within it.

Kindness costs nothing yet has unlimited rewards.

JULY 11

CHEMISTRY
The interaction of one personality with another

The world is abundant with perspectives and personalities at over seven billion inhabitants and counting. Some personalities can clash with others, however, we must remember that all relationships improve when both parties work to establish and maintain solidarity. Even within the family structure or group, working to have good chemistry is important. This helps to create more fluid experiences for the members when problem solving or pursuing goals.

The potential output increases as a group's chemistry develops.

JULY 12

WOMEN
Adult female humans

Many people over time have stated that they do not understand women. In order to understand them, one must take the time to consider their needs and the way they operate. Generally, the necessities for women include security, comfortable environments and meaningful relationships. They are emotional thinkers, so they may be more inclined to process information based on how they feel. Such a quality is valuable because instincts are powerful indicators revealing the needed insight toward accomplishing a goal. The power of the woman is maximized when there is a healthy balance of instinct and logic to optimize decision-making.

Women give the precious gift of perspective to the world, so listen closely.

JULY 13

MARRIAGE
The formal union recognized by law

The essence of marriage lives in strength of the honest partnership between the couple. The potential for disagreements will occur as long as you are dealing with any two people. If the couple looks toward each other as the source of the problem, negative energy and attitudes will grow. However, if both share the philosophy to work together toward the challenges or issues, life and home become much easier to manage. Effective communication is the cornerstone for all happy and successful marriages.

Honor your marriage to inspire others to want the same.

JULY 14

DISCRETION
The quality of behaving or speaking in such a way as to avoid causing offense or revealing private information.

Your name and your word are the only things that are truly yours in this world. The quality of them creates your reputation. The way you are known in society will dictate the opportunities that will be presented to you. People will not trust you if you are known for being lazy. In contrast, if you are known for being wise and truthful, people will approach you for sound advice. We all have shortcomings, but be aware and careful who you tell them to so you do not damage your reputation.

Do not broadcast every detail of your life for the public to see.

JULY 15

RECIPROCITY
A relation of mutual dependence or action or influence

The universe is built in such a way that energy is in constant flow. I remember a time when I was in an emotionally negative place in life. I felt overwhelmed by the challenges of my life and was more sensitive to the negativity around. My focus was misplaced. It was a blessing that the people around me poured positivity and encouragement into my life. They initiated and nurtured my physical and emotional healing. Since I have overcome those personal challenges, it is my responsibility to help the world do the same.

The energy that you invest in the world will be the same as what you will receive.

JULY 16

ARCHITECT
The deviser, maker, or creator of anything

Human nature compels us to build and use creativity to enhance the quality of existing creations. Oftentimes, one aspect is overlooked – our relationships. What are we doing to establish and cultivate our relationships with others? Have any of our actions resulted in damage toward a relationship? The seeds of our interactions must be handled in a delicate manner so they can bloom into life long associations. Problems are solved much quicker when there is familiarity.

Building relationships is the key to successful resolutions.

JULY 17

ANNIVERSARY
The date on which an event took place in a previous year

You made it! You should embrace this important moment. Every passing year is a defining and notable bookmark in your life. This is a reflection of your persistence and durability. One of the toughest challenges for people is to continue to moving forward in pursuit of a goal. The anniversary can relate to instances such as relationships, job tenure or other facets. The more time you invest in an area, you increase your value within the scope of the area. Relish this moment and remember you are much more valuable than you think. Congratulations!

Every anniversary marks a milestone accomplished.

JULY 18

ENCOURAGEMENT
The expression of approval and support

A gesture or word of encouragement is often the boost we need to move forward and accomplish our goals. We tend to work and perform better when we know there are people cheering for us. Positive energy is infectious. It is important for us to give encouragement to those around us because our words can help them through their key moments of struggle. At the same time, we must not forget that our self-talk must also be positive and encouraging so that we are more productive.

Your positive words breathe life into those in despair.

JULY 19

THOUGHTFUL
To show consideration for the needs of other people

The more thoughtful humanity is the more opportunities are created. Within the various networks of people, we hear about opportunities around us that we may not use, yet we can share with others. If we know of someone is in need and there is an opportunity for fulfillment, use the open lines of communication to inform others. When you inform others of opportunities, your neighbors will bestow the same favor unto you.

Consider how you can positively change the lives of others.

JULY 20

OATH
A solemn promise regarding one's future action or behavior

An oath resonates within us much deeper than a mere promise. A promise is just a vow to carry out a certain action. An oath reflects more on the philosophy responsible for your decision-making. Promises seemed to buckle under the pressure of time constraints or lack of availability. Oaths, however, are thought to be much more serious and of the utmost priority, thus making them more noble. The underlying foundation of this is the quality and reliability of your word. What is the value of your word?

Someone's life may depend on the oath you make.

JULY 21

PUNISHMENT
The infliction of a penalty as retribution for an offense

In all types of relationships, you could encounter a wrongdoing toward you. The pain and strife associated with the offense can make you want revenge at all costs whether deliberate or unintentional. Vengeance not worth your time nor energy. The universe has established the karmic process of justice. It is your place to defend yourself always but not in a vengeful or vindictive mode. Such reactions will only drain your essence and zest for life which will leave you empty in every aspect.

Those who wrong you will always get what they deserve.

JULY 22

BONDS
Something, as an agreement or friendship, which unites individuals or people into a group; a covenant

Evaluate your relationships and note which stand out. The bonds with others can be established through schooling, sports, events or other life experiences. Even in the midst of unfortunate or even tragic situations, good things can arise from such challenges like the stronger bonds between those involved. These moments, at times, are the most memorable bonds because they are forged in the fires of suffering and despair. Bonds are often the catalysts for lifelong friendships.

Establish bonds that are fruitful and pure.

JULY 23

MEN
Adult human male

Men are much simpler than people think. In general, guys are practical thinkers, so they are more concerned about the actions to be addressed and the tasks to be completed. This creates of tunnel vision to prioritize the factors necessary to make sound decisions. The way men analyze information is commonly directed toward what needs to be done. The male's logical mind is concerned with conquering tasks and circumstances, which is why there is such a strong connection with men and sports. The male who can maximize his logical thinking and understand the emotional side of life is a prime commodity. Such men are highly regarded – which is why they are called gentlemen. This is the target to pursue.

*The quality of your manhood is measured from
the chest-up, not the waist-down.*

JULY 24

TENSION
Mental or emotional strain

In conflicts with others, finding common ground is key to resolving the outstanding issues. How can one be effective in reaching this end? The answer is similar to when in negotiations – take your feelings out of the equation. You then can think more logically about whether the mutually beneficial result is attainable or not. Be inspired by your passions to create your negotiating stance, however, balance your reasoning with practical thinking to better process the information.

*Remove emotion from confrontations
to arrive at a quicker resolution.*

JULY 25

UNITY
Harmony or agreement between people or groups

I can never accomplish as much as WE can. With others, more work is assumed and more tasks are accomplished. For larger goals to be reached I need you as much as you need me. I can only do a little when alone. My energy and my vision are limited to my capabilities on any particular day. On the other hand, if WE can manage to work in unison and stand united in our cause, there is no limit to what WE can conquer together.

The shared vision of moving toward the same goal is the most important trait of a team.

JULY 26

PASSION
Any powerful or compelling emotion or feeling

The things that we are passionate about can cause both joy and despair when out of control. The love we have within us is what makes us human. Our hearts energize the battery of humanity. We must direct those feelings well and manage them logically so we do not cause harm to others or ourselves. The love we share is best when used toward the development of others. We then can inspire people to love one another as we are built to do.

Love is a sacred gift that connects the world together.

JULY 27

FELLOWSHIP

Mutual trust and friendship among people who spend time together.

Within your social circles, you will encounter people with various interests and abilities. These are very important people to have in your corner. Some moments you will need to consult with them for advice or even ask for the expertise in an area in which you are unfamiliar. Moving through life, you will find them as valuable contributors to your success, so you must be there for them in the same manner.

Camaraderie bestows energy to the weary and comfort to the burdened.

JULY 28

BAGGAGE

Things that encumber one's freedom, progress or development

At times, a close relationship may not end well. The two most common areas affected by such a situation are trust and self-esteem. Some people have problems trusting the next person for what another in the past has done. Do not miss the new blessing because of old circumstances. Do not give fresh power to past despair. You are much better than this. View each situation separately and treat people with fairness. Most importantly, when a relationship is over, close the door behind it.

During the journey of any relationship, be sure to travel light.

JULY 29

COMPATABILITY

Capable of existing or performing in harmonious, agreeable,
or congenial combination with another or others

Life moves and evolves to maintain its fluid nature. Essentially, life is a peaceful journey until incompatible pieces are encountered. Roadblocks of poor decisions and potholes of unfruitful people make the journey rocky and can cause major detours. Be careful of what situations and people you introduce into your life because those who are incompatible with your pursuits will cause more energy and time to be lost.

In the puzzle of life, some pieces will not always fit where you want them.

JULY 30

SERVICE

The action of helping or doing work for someone

Those who serve others understand a valuable lesson in life – humanity is maximized through service. This concept has been passed through generations and is applicable today. We must continue to work together and do for each other because there may not always be a time when we can care for ourselves. Always see opportunities to serve others, even in small ways. The task may seem insignificant but your impact will be irreplaceable.

Dedication to service will open the many doors of opportunity.

JULY 31

RELATIONSHIPS

The way in which two or more concepts, objects, or
people are connected, or the state of being connected

In whom do you invest your time and energy? To live a prosperous life, foster meaningful relationships with everyone who you contact. Such actions do not guarantee that you will best friends with everyone. This shows your understanding of people's value and their importance to your development. Whether connecting with family, friends, colleagues or associates, the relationships that you cultivate will have a direct correlation to the strength of your support system and the success that you can achieve.

*The quality of your social circles
affects the fruitfulness of your life.*

AUGUST

BUILDING WEALTH

How does wealth relate to your connections? Wealth is created by having a financial vehicle (i.e. products, services, investments) and, most importantly, people. Without your connections to the people, no finances nor value is transferred. To build wealth of all types, you much be in touch with the pulse of humanity. As you interact with humanity, you will be rewarded in kind.

AUGUST 1

COMPETITION
The rivalry for supremacy

Without competition, you cannot discover your strengths and weaknesses. Competition is not limited to ideas of winning and losing. Your development is crucial. Your competitors are necessary to your future achievements whether in a contest or running a business. They are important for you to realize what you must invest to reach the level of success you desire.

Healthy competition brings out the best in everyone.

AUGUST 2

PRIORITIES
The fact or condition of being regarded or treated as more important

In order to build wealth, you must establish your priorities. Unless you possess an infinite amount of resources, you must plan and be wise in execution to maximize the results of your efforts. In the framework of your goals, what are the most important items to consider? What details are essential to set a strong foundation for your success? Questions such as these will help you to give you a more clear direction toward your goals.

The better you manage the critical areas
the sooner your path is revealed.

AUGUST 3

SYSTEMS

A set of detailed methods, procedures, and routines established or formulated to carry out a specific activity, perform a duty, or solve a problem.

Each aspect of life is a product of a system. This includes all tangible and abstract things. To be a doctor, I must follow the system of proper schooling, residency and perform well on necessary exams. To build a home, I must lay a strong foundation, setup the framing and then use materials for completion. All of our aspirations work in the same manner. For whatever you want to become or achieve, when you follow the actions within the system, you are more likely for success.

Learn how to operate the system to get what you desire from it.

AUGUST 4

BUSINESS

A person's regular occupation, profession, or trade

Those with unique ideas or special skills often create businesses with hopes to increase their wealth. In a time when advertisements are literally everywhere, some people do anything to encourage the use of products or services. Sometimes, they will resort to illegal or immoral means so their business makes the most money possible. There is always a proper and noble way to achieve wealth. Invest your energy into the items that help people. Focus on the well-being of the people and your brand will reflect all that is honorable and good.

Provide products and services to improve people without exploiting them.

AUGUST 5

PERSUATION
The act of influencing to reach a desired end

Persuasion is not to be used to manipulate people for selfish gain. In this case, it is used to deliver a message to others when your ideas are based in truth and your proven philosophy is beneficial to the listeners. No matter how astounding the message, patience is a key factor of persuading someone to see a situation through your perspective. Appropriate timing makes a huge difference as well. People will never change their thinking unless they are open to the change. If they are not, wait until they are more willing to hear the message you are trying to convey.

Convince the people of how your ideas benefit them much more than you.

AUGUST 6

COMPLETE
Finish making or doing

In order to obtain more, some think you must <u>do</u> more, yet this is not entirely true. To be the most efficient, you must finish one project before moving on to the next. To have more of anything, you must <u>finish</u> more. Anyone can be busy with on-going tasks and actions. When items are completed, however, the result is a valuable product. To build wealth of all types involves the creation of finished products to then be marketed for financial gain.

Your finished products determine the size of your gain.

AUGUST 7

WEALTH

An abundance of valuable material possessions or resources

Real wealth is not confined to a number of items you possess and is not limited to the financial realm. We are created to be wealthy in every area of our lives, including in physical and emotional areas. Physical wealth relates to the proper health and wellness that we must work to maximize to the best of our ability. Emotional wealth is derived from the strength of our self-esteem and the quality of our relationships. Our overall quality of life improves drastically when each of these areas is addressed.

The purpose of wealth is to teach us how to bestow resources to others charitably.

AUGUST 8

VOCATION

A person's employment or main occupation regarded as worthy and requiring much dedication

Decisions about a job path can be overwhelming. Many jobs available can make us a lot of money, however only a relative few can give us fulfillment. To find this, we must look within to examine the hobbies we love and the concepts that we find most interesting. Each of us have a natural trade to be used to make a living.

Find a beloved craft and you will never work a day in your life.

AUGUST 9

LUXURY
Something inessential but conducive to pleasure and comfort

Nothing is wrong with having luxurious things as long as they do not define who you are as a person. It is good to aspire to own nice things but if you emotionally tie yourself to such objects, you will slowly lose your common touch of humanity. The judgment of others based on the luxuries they possess is very misleading because character and expensive items have no relationship. Prices can often be changed, yet having wealth of character should always be a constant pursuit.

One's value never equals the total price of possessions.

AUGUST 10

VALUE
Relative worth, merit, or importance

Life moves fast and creates the challenge to keep track of our daily affairs. Moments may leave us wondering how we got into that situation or circumstance. We must continue to remind ourselves that for each condition and occurrence, we have given it permission to reside in our lives, which includes both positive and negative aspects. The more attention paid to a situation, the more life we breathe into it, which allows it to remain present in our lives longer.

Add things to your life with high value instead of high cost.

AUGUST 11

POVERTY
The state of being inferior in quality or insufficient in amount

Oftentimes, poverty refers to insufficient finances; however, there are conditions that are more unfortunate. If you gladly accepted a life that you do not want, then you are living in poverty. If you feel as though you are tied to people who only drain your positive energy, then you are living in poverty. Even some of the wealthiest people on earth live in mental poverty. All of the above people maintain the potential to do anything, yet they refuse to change the circumstances due to one of many types of fear. Be bold and pursue the life that you desire.

Poverty of the mind has more devastating effects than the lack of money.

AUGUST 12

ECONOMICS
The branch of knowledge concerned with the production, consumption, and transfer of wealth

The understanding of economics to create financial wealth extends beyond the ideas of supply and demand. To create profitable situations, there will be an opportunity cost for what you are giving up. To maximize your productivity, visualize what would be your most desired result before you begin. Afterwards, decide which course of action leads you directly to your goals while using the least in resources.

Always expect to give something in order to get something.

AUGUST 13

SPEED
Rapidity of movement or action

Riches can be achieved overnight by following what is temporarily popular. Vast wealth is accumulated over time. This blueprint for wealth has a direct correlation to the pursuit of all goals. To achieve enduring success, slow but steady advancements give you valuable experience to hold on to what you gain. The faster that you receive the spoils of your goal, the faster that they can be lost.

It is better to gradually achieve small goals than to reach a large one quickly.

AUGUST 14

APPRENTICE
A person who is learning a trade from a skilled employer, having agreed to work for a fixed period at low wages

Many areas of business in which you can be successful exist, but it will not happen overnight. In new situations, the beginning stage as an apprentice is the most critical. To become the CEO of a company, you must learn every aspect of what makes the company operate. Being a studious apprentice grants you experience on the proper execution of tasks while learning about the nature of the industry. Do not rush through this stage because you may miss essential ideas needed for later.

Humble yourself enough to crawl before you walk.

AUGUST 15

BUDGET

An estimate of income and expenditure for a set period of time

We are living in times when misuse of finances cause major disruptions and stress in people's lives. Determine how to spend your resources and make a budget to have a clear sense of your financial health. Life will always introduce situations causing you to use your resources unexpectedly. Budget well and have a plan of action to make better decisions to minimize the impact from life's surprise attacks.

Avoid spending money that you do not actually possess.

AUGUST 16

NEGOTIATE

An attempt to reach an agreement or compromise by discussion

Everyone has a price whether of monetary or conceptual value. People are open to negotiation when they realize such value. The key is for them understand what must be given up to receive some benefit. In your dealings with people, put yourself in their shoes. Understand the elements driving them and you will gain a sense of what they value as rewards. By knowing such information, you will be empowered to recognize mutually favorable terms to get what you want by creating win-win situations.

Find the right conditions and people will respond in your favor.

AUGUST 17

WAITING

Stay where one is or delay action until a particular
time or until something else happens

When imagining someone who appears to be waiting, we often think of very serene picture of a person sitting. The most dangerous hindrance to all progress resides within such a picture. Waiting is not to be done passively as if a miraculous event will happen just because you hope it will. Those who have mastered the art of waiting are wise with their time because they continue to plan and execute the necessary steps toward reaching the goal simultaneously. Waiting is about using all of your time and energy to the maximum and then allowing the results to unfold.

The mastery of waiting is not achieved by standing still.

AUGUST 18

EMPLOYMENT

A person's trade or profession

All employment has nobility included. To complete work and deliver a job well done is a direct reflection of your skills, determination and creativity. In addition, there is much trust involved for those in power to bestow responsibilities upon you. They determined that you were more than qualified to accept and complete tasks given to you. What they have given you is not just work, rather an opportunity to excel one task at a time.

The quality of your work says more about you than your words.

AUGUST 19

CAREER
A person's trade or profession

When searching for the right career, you must look for the careers proven to make money over time. Doctors, firefighters and lawyers continue to thrive in their respective industries. For doctors, or anyone in medicine related fields, there will always be people to become ill, fires will always occur and there will always be the need for those who interpret the law. With time, if you recognize an opportunity to create a new type of career, consider how many people could use your services and how often they come back.

Seek a career in a field with a track record of longevity.

AUGUST 20

ALLOCATE
Distribute resources or duties for a particular purpose

Resources can be difficult to gather or create. For this reason, do not be wasteful with them. You must treat your resources with care and divide them wisely to receive some type of benefit, whether monetary or otherwise. For anything that you invest, aim to receive more than what you initially invested. This mindset will give you the mental flexibility to analyze each investment opportunity to increase the likelihood of being profitable.

Distribute your resources accordingly to reap the most benefits.

AUGUST 21

FIDELITY

Faithfulness to a person, cause, or belief, demonstrated by continuing loyalty and support

For the people who worked hard to build their fortunes, sometimes they had to perform all of the jobs necessary to become successful. This idea is especially true with new and/or growing companies. Oftentimes, the business owners must fight against all of the challenges of home and remain faithful to the reason why they wanted to create the business is the first place. Similar to any goal, you must believe in yourself and be loyal to your calling. The thirst for money can lead to wasted time. The following of these intangibles will fill the void that extends well beyond money.

Success is determined by your commitment to executing the necessary tasks.

AUGUST 22

PROFIT

Obtain a financial advantage or benefit from an investment

We are made to create and manage in every aspect of our lives. During the flow of this unending cycle, our energy and resources are in constant and dynamic movement. The decisions we make regarding where to place the energy and resources should always be on the side of profit. This does not mean we should disregard the value of others nor do them any harm. In all undertakings, we should perform tasks that are financially favorable and teach others how to do the same.

Allow every action to benefit you in some way.

AUGUST 23

INNOVATION
A new method, idea or product

The pursuit of all goals includes some type of system. Learn the series of steps needed to achieve the consistent results, however do not be exclusively bound to it. Every system is open for improvement. Use your creativity to discover methods to reduce the number of steps to improve your process efficiency or increase the product quality. In some cases, these new processes can inspire completely new products or services to be created. Innovation has proven to change our technological world. What areas could benefit from innovation in your life?

Innovation is the art of learning the rules, breaking them and getting something better than you expected.

AUGUST 24

AGENDA
A list of items of business to be considered and discussed at a meeting

In the business world, meetings are full of agendas. The facilitator of the meeting strives to meet every topical requirement based on the time constraints, if any. Our lives operate in the same fashion. Each day must include a personal agenda written to maximize the time we possess. Document your plans so they become a piece of the physical world and a powerful extension of your thoughts.

Make a tentative plan for each day to keep you on track.

AUGUST 25

CAPITALIZE

Take the chance to gain advantage from

To be profitable is typically the #1 goal of all businesses. As you live in a capitalistic society, you may find that the concepts essential to business success can be used to enjoy a successful life. Everything you do can be interpreted as a short term or long-term investment. If you begin a workout routine, expect to have better health and flexibility. If you begin learning how to play chess, aim to master the skills and eventually defeat your teacher. In each of these examples, you must invest time and discipline to reach a desired results.

With every decision, be sure to gain more than you lose.

AUGUST 26

FINANCES

The conduct or transaction of money matters generally

Financial resources are an important aspect to your overall life. Access to them gives you more immediate options choose from based on your purchasing power. By cash, credit or financial assets, like stocks and bonds, your decision-making skills regarding your finances must be well developed. In most cases, if you want to discover what you value, watch how you spend your money. As you operate your own business or simply manage your household, this information will help guide your actions to become more profitable.

Manage your money well to obtain peace of mind.

AUGUST 27

FRUGAL
Simple and plain and costing little

The primary trait of the wealthy is to be frugal. Of course, there will be moments when they will make big-ticket purchases, yet their philosophy involves practical decision-making. Compare two items of equal quality and one will cost $1,000 while the other is $200. Why choose the higher priced one simply due to a brand name? The savings of $800 can be used in more ways that are productive rather than paying for a popular name of a product.

The foolish spend to satisfy the ego while the wise spend based on the utility of items.

AUGUST 28

CREDIT
The ability to obtain goods or services before payment, based on the trust that payment will be made in the future

Credit is commonly used for an emergency, home or vehicle purchases. The misuse of credit to buy frivolous items of no practical value gives little benefit beyond the ability to show off your new stuff. The use of credit is good only when is managed well through your budget. If not used properly, it can be detrimental to your financial health. To reap the most benefit, pay the bills in full as soon as they are due to build your credit score and create an increase in purchasing power.

Wisdom with credit accelerates the attainment of wealth.

AUGUST 29

HONOR
To regard with much respect

The way in which you conduct business is often the mirror of your character. If you are dishonest during business related interactions or negotiations, the same dishonesty is most likely present within the framework of your personality. As you run your daily business affairs, remember the same effort in energy you invest it to become a honorable person is also needed to ensure that your business decisions and products reflect upright intentions.

Perform every duty as if it were to be judged by an expert.

AUGUST 30

PRODUCTIVE
To possess the power to create results

Whether focused on one goal or working toward a few at a time, mark the completion of each stage with a physical representation. For example when working on writing project, celebrate the completion of each part. Create a visual depiction such as a graph or make an event of it, such as treating yourself to a special dinner. Each small reward creates a tangible reminder of your consistency and productive direction of completing the necessary stages of your goal. Such positive energy and current sense of accomplishment will thrust you toward your finish line.

Evidence of your efforts will give you encouragement to finish.

AUGUST 31

MONEY

A current medium of exchange in the form of coins and banknotes

Money is the most powerful tool in existence. If there is too little of it, a life can become bitter environment. If there is too much of it, one can become delusional and unkind. Money is also a tool of inspiration for people to make better lives for themselves when used properly. Through such people, charitable organizations and wealth-generating opportunities can be created so others can use their intellect and determination to achieve financial freedom. Financial resources and available time are the factors determining how much wealth you possess.

*Use money as a vehicle to free your time -
not as a tool to get the most toys.*

MASTERING YOUR POWER

The final stage of peace comes full circle. After learning the truth about yourself and how to manage the interactions with others, you will examine how to maximize today's power to begin fulfilling your purpose. You then can direct this profound energy to create joyful experiences while building the productive life that you desire. When you possess everlasting hope, you can achieve all things.

SEPTEMBER

THE GIFT OF NOW

Most of us place emphasis on the possibilities for tomorrow. Looking forward is a good practice but it alone is not enough. What can you do today to improve your chances of success for tomorrow? There is always room for patience, but none for procrastination. Right now is the most important moment in your life.

SEPTEMBER 1

TODAY
On or in the course of this present day

Every sunrise gives birth to opportunity. You have the chance to correct the shortcomings of yesterday. Your energy is renewed to take on tasks of the day. Yesterday has gone. The only purpose the past serves is to motivate you for today. You must walk with purpose and work with urgency because the most important moments of your life just arrived. Your goals are waiting patiently for you to attain them. What are you doing with your "now"?

Today marks the dawn of a new beginning.

SEPTEMBER 2

STEADFAST
Resolutely or dutifully firm and unwavering

Your decision-making skills are more important than ever. Do not let anyone change your mind when you decide to pursue a goal. Stand by your decision if you considered all of the needed resources and weighed all of the options. You are the master of your fate. Listen to the advice of trusted people but do not be easily swayed by public opinion. Your strength of thought is your foundation.

Let nothing hinder you from fulfilling the purpose of your day.

SEPTEMBER 3

CALCULATE
Determine by sound reasoning or experience

You must focus right now on executing yesterday's plans to reach tomorrow's accomplishment. Every large undertaking is nothing more than a collection of smaller tasks. Perform each task using the least amount of our resources and energy necessary to create the results you want. Follow the same pattern for each task so you create small but measurable steps to reach the overall goal. Calculate your steps of advancement to consider each option available to you and choose what makes the most productive sense.

Planning is the priority of every journey.

SEPTEMBER 4

WORK
Activity involving mental or physical effort to achieve a result

The fundamental equation of work is time + effort = results. We are action-oriented beings and possess the ability to work in some capacity. Right now, others are working toward the goals that you want to achieve. They are patiently preparing themselves to perform at the highest level when the opportunity arrives. Are you working just as diligently, if not more? Encounters of success do not happen as a matter of chance or magic. They are a direct reflection of your work ethic. The floodgates of opportunity will open for you when your work ethic is strong. View your small progressions as major accomplishments.

If your results are not satisfactory, adjust your work habits.

SEPTEMBER 5

ADVOCATE
Publicly recommend or support

We live in a world that appears to be accepting of negativity and injustice. Soon, we must choose our stance on an issue and defend it when we know we are right. People will differ in opinions of what makes our world better, yet a common thread of joy is what we all hope to attain. This joy is discovered when there is peace amongst the people. In short, when you support the factors that foster peace, humanity will continue to advance.

Make sure your voice is heard when truth and justice are on your side.

SEPTEMBER 6

CAUTION
Care taken to avoid danger or mistakes

This moment is much too important to take lightly. There is no time for reckless behavior. In the actions you take and situations you encounter, you must be wise. This does not mean you should be fearful at any point. Rather, should take the time to think situations through before you jump into them with all of your energy and resources. When you view the full picture of the opportunities for you, you can recognize possible problems and avoid them.

It does not make sense to run with your eyes closed.

SEPTEMBER 7

BOLDNESS
Being without hesitation or fear in the face of danger

A hammer is used when we must work with nails. A screwdriver must be used when setting screws. Neither of these tools is as effective when performing a task different from what they were made for. People operate in the same fashion. Our skills and attributes are unique to the purposes we are to fulfill. The beauty of the situation is that we own the ability and the right to define our purpose. We must understand the power to choose resides within us and that power cannot be taken away.

There are tasks that only you are meant to fulfill.

SEPTEMBER 8

NO
Rejection or a negative answer

"NO" is the most important word in your development. It is often connected with negative feelings or subordination but they can provide valuable information about your skills or progress. "No" provides instant feedback regarding IF a skill or performance standard is met. The only way to improve is to expose your shortcomings so you can make the proper adjustments. "No" is also important to give the feedback necessary for others to grow. Those who avoid saying no to others seldom give good advice because they have not established a standard of excellence.

Every "No" teaches you how to get to the "Yes".

SEPTEMBER 9

CHALLENGES
A call or summons to engage in any contest

Challenges are the "meat & potatoes" of life. A majority of our daily interaction involves working through, giving assistance with, or celebrating the conquering of our challenges. The best parts of challenging situations are the lessons learned along the way. These are essential for us to grow as professionals and as people. All challenges serve as testing grounds for you to show what you are capable of doing. You must maximize these opportunities and always do your best.

The results of your current challenges will create your next opportunity.

SEPTEMBER 10

GIFT
A special aptitude, ability or power

We all possess some kind of gift. Whether special ability of action or thought, it also must be discovered and nurtured to grow as a seed of opportunity. Identify the concepts and items to which you show the most passion when searching for your gift. Then consider the actions that you perform exceptionally well. This consideration will uncover the multiple paths of life options used to create your destiny. Invest energy toward your gifted area and you will inspire others. This teaches them to be the best within their gifts as well.

To use your gifts to uplift humanity is the most honorable duty of all.

SEPTEMBER 11

SINCERITY

To be genuine; not hypocritical or deceitful

Each moment is precious and requires your full attention. You will use your energy based on information from others, so you must evaluate their level of sincerity. Surround yourself with people who are consistent in telling you the truth, regardless of whether they benefit or not. These people add the valuable perspective that can be used to broaden current ideas and help you to see potential problems ahead of time. Sincerity is all about giving and receiving direct and honest information to help others make better quality decisions.

The truth of your intentions will shine through your actions.

SEPTEMBER 12

IMPULSE

A sudden strong urge or desire to act

We live in a world where the people are poisoned by instant gratification. Our desires, at times, will not come as quickly as expected. Some of us will dismiss our goals because we believe that since success has not happened yet, it never will happen. This is an unstable philosophy to possess. We must avoid giving a mindless reaction based on our natural urges. If we move too quickly, we will restrict or even remove our logical thinking from the decision-making equation. To act with impulse is costly and sometimes dangerous. We must be decisive after weighing our options, yet avoid procrastination.

Your mind is much more powerful than the sum of your urges.

SEPTEMBER 13

CATALOG

Make a systematic list of similar items

Write down any goals you want to reach. An amazing thing happens as soon as your pen or pencil hits the paper. Your ideas are potent. Once you write down your desired task, the concept moves from the idea world to the physical world. What lies on the page is the first visual representation of your thoughts. At this point, the most difficult part is over. Your actions convert this documented concept into a workable strategy to be accomplished.

If it is not written down, it probably will not happen.

SEPTEMBER 14

GRATITUDE

Readiness to show appreciation for and to return kindness

People who consistently make proper choices are often overlooked. Others expect this behavior and forget the importance of acknowledging the behavior. People will only continue to do positively reinforced acts. When a child performs an action that they should not do, usually some type of behavior modification takes place. However, if the same child performs a good action and receives some level of positive reinforcement, the likelihood of him or her repeating the action increases. We as adults respond the same when we consider our own habits.

Show people that you appreciate them for their goodness.

SEPTEMBER 15

INFLUENCE
The capacity to have an effect on the character,
development, or behavior of someone or something

You have no idea how powerful you are. When you have confidence in yourself and believe in a certain truth, you reach a level of understanding that most people merely wish they possessed. Some people have supreme confidence yet they lack ideas. Others are full of wholehearted beliefs, except in themselves. You, however, are different. Everyone can see it. Your aura emits a unique and undeniable energy. The public is drawn to you in hopes of hearing how you attain peace in your life that they desperately seek. This is the source of your power. Now, what will you do with it?

You are the catalyst for a revolution.

SEPTEMBER 16

FORGIVENESS
To excuse for a fault or offense; pardon

In some moments, people will do what they think is best for themselves and neglect your needs. The neglect may be intentional or accidental but you must forgive others for their transgressions. The most important person you must forgive is yourself. None of us are perfect, yet we can strive to minimize our shortcomings. Life becomes bitter and cold which without forgiveness only grows into hatred. There is no room in life for hate. Forgiveness benefits the giver much more than the receiver and, therefore, liberates everyone.

*Bitterness is nothing more than an unlocked cage
that you can leave when you so choose.*

SEPTEMBER 17

DREAMS
An aspiration, goal or aim

Dreams are the snapshots of the future. Every successful person in history began with one single idea – a dream. Let no one discourage you from them. Dreams are amazing because they appear to you when you already have access to the tools needed to bring it into fruition. When time and a strong work ethic are added to such ideas, dreams become reality. Do not seek acceptance or permission from others regarding your dreams because is your responsibility to achieve it.

The fine line separating dreams and reality depends on whether we drew it with pencil or pen.

SEPTEMBER 18

GARBAGE
A thing considered worthless or meaningless

Garbage is one of the main things in which people struggle to identify. Many would rather continue living with situations and people who do not benefit them at all rather than disposing of them. When people become comfortable with things giving no additional value, their life becomes busy and cluttered. Much energy is spent trying to make unfruitful things become productive which only drains your resources. Everything has an expiration date, so you must concern yourself only with useful things and recognize when their time has come to an end.

What does you no good must be thrown away.

SEPTEMBER 19

ADVERSARY

One's opponent in a contest, conflict or dispute

Many people believe that having an adversary is a naturally bad thing. They view opposition as something to overcome or defeat in order to reach their goals. Take your focus away from your opposition and consider them as a mirror to reveal your weaknesses. The sooner you realize your shortcomings, you can address them to improve yourself. Similar to a sporting event, you can plan before the competition begins, yet some of the most crucial adjustments will occur during the event itself. An adversary forces you to maximize your preparation and decision-making skills to be the most successful. If you master self-examination, the victory will be yours regardless of who opposes you.

Those who challenge you exist to improve your skills.

SEPTEMBER 20

COMPARE

To estimate, measure, or note the similarity or dissimilarity between

Making comparisons can be a great measuring tool when done properly. Sometimes, when we rate ourselves by the standards of others, we are left lost and frustrated because we are essentially comparing apples to oranges. The key is to compare you to yourself. Take everything about who you are today and compare that to the vision of yourself after you achieve your goal. The differences between these two people are the ideas that you must cultivate. Everyday your work should involve small steps to decrease the distance between where you are now and who you aspire to be. You are much closer than you think.

Take the time to compare your options thoroughly before making decisions.

SEPTEMBER 21

SIMPLICITY

The quality or condition of being easy to understand or do

People often mistake activity for importance. Life is, however, as simple as placing one foot in front of the other. Do not overwhelm yourself with an abundance of tasks. This is the easiest way for life to box you in. Focus on addressing one task at a time. This is all you can manage well at any given moment. Thinking with simplicity does not mean to overlook important ideas and challenges. Filter those ideas down to the essential decision-making moments by removing the blinding glamour or complex details around it.

Do not make life more difficult – be a master of simplicity.

SEPTEMBER 22

PARTICIPATION

The act of sharing in the activities of a group

The people who give the most knowledge about an activity are those directly engaged. Someone can read numerous volumes written or watch countless hours of others but they still will be missing the noteworthy pieces gained by experience. Whether competing in an academic contest, sporting event, or other task, the participants are viewed as the masters of their craft. Your hands-on experience will open up a vast number of opportunities. Venture out and explore new areas so you can determine what activities will receive your energetic attention.

Experience removes doubt from your life's equation.

SEPTEMBER 23

CURIOSITY
A strong desire to know or learn something

The asking of questions is a simple but powerful tool used to accelerate your development. For every question, at least one definite answer exists. In addition, all questions have been asked before. Your job simply becomes asking the right questions to get the right answers. In a career, your curiosity will dictate your level of success. The more passionately inquisitive you are about a topic and the more information you receive, the better you will understand the relationship of its inner and outer working parts. When you understand the relationships, the pieces become easier to control.

Never be afraid to dive into the seas of uncharted waters.

SEPTEMBER 24

READINESS
The state of being fully prepared for something

To be ready has nothing to do with being tense with anticipation. It means having comfort to know that whatever happens, you can act to maximize your window of opportunity. In order to maintain readiness, you must be a resoundingly calm to make intelligent decisions. You must be acutely aware so you are sensitive enough to notice when the hint of an opportunity presents itself. When you are consistently ready, you are poised under pressure because you are prepared for whatever may arise.

Think quickly and act upon whatever may come.

SEPTEMBER 25

PROBABILITY
A strong likelihood or chance of an occurrence

In life, there will always be good and bad situations to occur. The concept of karma plays a huge role in our existence. You reap what you sow. In other words, your outward actions determine what life experiences come back toward you. If you want to grow a garden, you must plant seeds. If you want to pass an academic exam, you must study the covered material. If you want to be treated well and respected by others, you must do this also. Decide what you want from life and when you "become" it, you will receive it.

Circumstances are more likely to go in your favor when you do good deeds.

SEPTEMBER 26

SHORTCUT
An alternative route believed to be faster than the one usually taken

Seek advantages for the opportunities presented to you but avoid shortcuts. To take a shortcut is very different from acting efficiently. Efficiency involves having the resources and skills to do what needs to be done. Shortcuts put you in a beneficial position without having the knowledge, skills or ability to maintain your position. Shortcuts can be detrimental to your aspirations because they do not add anything valuable to your development. It is better to take the time to reach your goals and keep it, rather than reach success and quickly lose the benefits.

One cannot appreciate the scenic route when moving too fast.

SEPTEMBER 27

APPLICATION
The act of putting to a special use or purpose

All knowledge is to be applied in some form or fashion. Having a vast number of dynamic ideas is great but not by itself. Ideas without actions applied will never be fruitful. To take actions without well-planned ideas only makes you busy and constantly frustrated at the lack of progress. There must be a balance of ideas and application for you to be successful. A constant flow must exist which includes brainstorming, planning and execution of such ideas. After the execution phase, you should evaluate the results and begin the process again. Your added energy will bring you closer to your goal.

Application is the life-giving force for knowledge.

SEPTEMBER 28

BIRTHDAY
The day of one's birth

Every year, you have at least one day to call your own. On this day, you can celebrate yourself and be reminded to treat yourself once in awhile. It's your birthday! This annual reminder serves to mark another year of your personal growth. It is also an indicator of the relationships you have developed. This personal "New Year" gives you a fresh start. This is the time to decide what will be your new set of goals. What adventure would you like to conquer in this New Year of Life?

Celebrate all that you have overcome in the last year.

SEPTEMBER 29

PRESENCE

The state or fact of existing, occurring, or being in a place or thing

As you move, the world responds to you. Whether at work, home or running errands, your energy accompanies you each step of the way. This energy, sometimes visually referred to as your aura, has tangible effects on the people who you encounter. Simply upon entering a room, your presence is felt. If you are in a bad mood and carry negative energy, you will find faults everywhere. You will be more likely to cause a negative experience for yourself and others. Maintain a positive mood and be cordial in your interactions. People will see excellence in you, which will inspire goodness in everyone.

Let your presence be a blessing to others, not a burden.

SEPTEMBER 30

IMPROVISE

To invent, compose, or perform with little or no preparation

The road of success does not follow one set system. It leaves room for instances of dead ends, detours and other roadblocks. There is no way to predict the future yet we can train ourselves to cope with changes whether gradual or abrupt. In a sense, we must plan for change just in case. More importantly, our mentality must be dynamic enough to adjust to the changing factors on which we based our lives. Sometimes you must act and make do with what you have despite the circumstances.

Your most detailed plans are still tentative.

OCTOBER

DISCOVERING PURPOSE

The underlying question of our existence has baffled humanity for ages. Scholars have debated tirelessly and have reached no conclusion. Their opinion is not necessary – yours is. Reflection upon your talents and passions will point you into the direction of your destiny. Your purpose is defined by you and you alone.

OCTOBER 1

PHILOSOPHY
The study of the fundamental nature of
knowledge, reality & existence

The proper mentality is essential when striving for achievement. The ability to handle adversity well and maintain positive self-talk both stem from possessing a productive philosophy. In the search for or work toward your purpose in life, you are simultaneously in pursuit of your personal truth. What good things do you want in your life? What habits hinder your progress? The more you seek to understand the elements of life, the better your vision will become toward all of your experiences.

Always question until the truth is revealed.

OCTOBER 2

REASON
Think, understand, and form judgments by a process of logic

One of your most valuable assets is your ability to think in a critical fashion. The use of your reasoning must be logical to solve problems. Oftentimes, when we rush our decisions based on emotional thinking we do not fully consider all the possibilities available to us. Every issue we encounter has solutions included. When we consider our options and the resources we possess, the choice we must make for our greatest benefit will become clear.

To find your answers, take a moment to think situations through.

OCTOBER 3

DEVELOPMENT
The process of growth or advancement.

There are many types of development. The most common is the maturation process we experience from childhood to adulthood. This is a natural occurrence and does not require much of our involvement. Cognitive development works differently because it is a matter resulting from our choices. Life will present situations to us to test our decision-making skills. Development is essential to fulfilling our purpose. We must decide to grow into who we are meant to be.

To reach the next level of achievement, we must develop our skills beyond where they are now.

OCTOBER 4

TRIALS
The state of a person or thing being tried or tested; subjection to suffering or grievous experiences

Tests are a natural set of occurrences designed to indicate our readiness for particular level of performance or endurance. These often appear as hardships or challenges that we may struggle with and sometimes we may even fail at them. Nonetheless, the trials are meant to show you the strength you possess and the quality of your decision-making skills when under pressure. This snapshot of you now will help you to prepare for all challenges to come in your life.

Hardships of life always contain lessons to teach us what matters.

OCTOBER 5

GO
To move or proceed to or from something

What do you want to accomplish? What tasks are you meant to fulfill? Everything in the world is at your disposal. All information required to make your decisions and every procedure you must follow for success is before you. Tough times are a part of life. You must expect them but never let them stop you. The truth is nothing can stop you once you believe you can do anything.

You are the only one who can do what you are meant to do.

OCTOBER 6

ACCUMULATE
Gather or acquire an increasing number or quantity of

For the goals you are trying to accomplish, there will be much to learn. Some education will be on the job training, or other lessons will be the result of failures along the way. In either case, you must add valuable knowledge to consider and tools to add to your tool belt. With time, your resources will grow and you will possess more than what is needed. When coupled with patient actions, the world will become your oyster.

Gather the skills that set you apart from everyone else.

OCTOBER 7

IDEAL
To satisfy one's conception of what is perfect or most suitable

In pursuit of fulfilling your purpose, you will realize that it is not comprised of one, but many goals. Plan your steps and consider the ideal resources and circumstances that can lead you to your goals. These keep you on track and allow you to maximize your creativity, yet do not be bound exclusively by the ideals. Sometimes, you must build using worn out tools. Even when situations do not match with your ideal circumstances, you can still achieve all that you desire.

Never expect things to be perfect but know what is acceptable.

OCTOBER 8

WARNING
A statement or event indicating a possible or impending danger, problem, or other unpleasant situation

There are a few different, yet important ways of warning people of a bad decision or dangerous circumstance. Advice from others is the most common way, followed by our own logical thoughts. The last and often the most obscure, is our internal instinct – the gut feeling that we all possess. All of these methods steer us toward the right decision. When we adhere to them and make the proper decisions, we save our most valuable asset – time.

Listen to the voice telling you to stop, slow down or wait.

OCTOBER 9

CATEGORIZE
Place in a particular class or group

Life is a vast ocean of circumstances, opportunities and relationships. Our feelings at times will overlap. Frustration or anger, from work or school, can spread into home interactions and cause more problems. You must learn to compartmentalize your energy. Whatever happens at work, leave the energy at work. If there is a negative occurrence at home, leave such energy at home. The only exception is that all positive energy can be free to migrate across all categories of life experiences.

Use energy from one area of your life to empower another.

OCTOBER 10

PAIN
Physical or mental suffering or discomfort caused by illness or injury

Pain is one of the most common causes of goals unfulfilled. Physical pain can stop us in our tracks during our productive actions. It can be treated and can be better with time. Emotional pain is different because it holds the potential to stop you from living a purposeful life. The cure for emotional pain is twofold. First, extract a positive life lesson so you can improve lives by teaching others how to overcome the experience. Second, you must let it go. Let go of your emotional ties to the situation. Focus your energy and attention away from the pain and invest it into the improvement of your life.

Discomfort tells us when it is time to move forward or move away.

OCTOBER 11

HEROES
A person who is admired for courage or noble qualities

Heroes are those who sacrificed in some way in hopes of having an impact on someone's life. Movies and theatrical performances are not the only instances where heroes are found. In some cases, the hero, whether male or female, may affect the whole population of people through a courageous and selfless act. The beauty about life is that if we look close enough, we will observe heroes living among us. You may even see one in the mirror.

Whose actions inspire you to improve your life?

OCTOBER 12

EXPAND
Become or make larger or more extensive

We naturally want more resources as we learn about their value. When we find experiences that give us pleasure, we want to experience them more often. Our lives are dominated by the pursuit of having more. In order to possess more and do more, you must <u>add</u> more. Add more attributes and skills to yourself, if possible. When you are unable to do so, use what you have in different and creative ways to accomplish what needs to be done. In such a case, you have expanded the application of the resource. How much more could you handle in life?

Enlarge your domain and govern it wisely.

OCTOBER 13

TALENT
Natural aptitude or skill

Some believe that your talents naturally appear when you are young. Your talents actually will make themselves known throughout your lifetime. All of us are talented in some area. In most cases, people may not even realize their talents unless they are exposed to opportunities to try them or experience an instance requiring them. Do not hide your abundance of skills. Allow them to flourish. Use your talents to improve your condition and make the lives around you better.

Investing in your talents will lead you to your purpose in life.

OCTOBER 14

JUDGMENT
The forming of an opinion, estimate, notion, or conclusion from circumstances presented to the mind

The manner in which you judge people and situations will be important to keep you on your purposeful journey. Do not judge people as good or bad. People all over the world are the same. Judge their actions. We all have made mistakes, but if made repeatedly, it is no longer mistake. It is a habit. Judge the consistency of others. Do not waste time and energy on someone who consistently fails to complete assigned tasks. Make the decision to find someone reliable who can get the job done so you may rest a little easier.

Sound judgment is the cornerstone of peace.

OCTOBER 15

CONCENTRATION

The action or power of focusing one's attention or mental effort to deal with one particular thing above all others.

Life will bring a host of ideas, circumstances and options your way all at one time. This can be mentally exhausting. Place your attention in the right areas at the proper time and all things will flow much smoother. Deal with the one thing at a time above all others after your priorities are established. The more uninterrupted mental processing time given to a singular idea or action will grant you much better results than you imagined.

Free your mind of all things except for the task at hand.

OCTOBER 16

TRANQUILITY

Quality or state of being serene; calmness; peacefulness

For me, there is nothing more coming and relaxing than lying down on the beach listing to the ocean waves. Where do you find your moment of tranquility? For you, it can be a place or even a joyous past experience that puts a smile on your face. There will be some moments in life when you must mentally escape just to get through the day. Be sure to have these peaceful places ready to be used during challenging times.

Find a peaceful place to recover for the journey ahead.

OCTOBER 17

EXCUSES
An explanation put forward to defend or justify a fault or offense

...

No one has time for your excuses.

OCTOBER 18

PRIDE
A sense of pleasure from achievements

Feel good about yourself and all that you are able to accomplish. You must be the one who believes wholeheartedly in your all of your goals. When they are achieved, do not think you are better than others because they have not experienced your level of success. Have pride in your work to reach a balanced self-esteem. Too much pride distances you from humanity and damages relationships. Just like riding a bike, you must maintain a balance in all times.

Never allow your pride to taint your self-image.

OCTOBER 19

STYLE
A manner of doing something

In an active life, you are guaranteed to both win and lose. You will experience positive and negative occurrences. How do you respond to such events? This response reflects your style. The manner in which you consistently respond to every aspect in life gives those looking up to you the permission to do the same. Be careful because your actions are speaking louder than you think. Your reactions shape the mindset of those after you.

What impression do you leave with people when you win or lose?

OCTOBER 20

FAILURE
Lack of success

The most successful people in the history of the world are often those who have failed the most. You cannot experience one without the other. They are linked with the bond that can never be broken – the bond of perspective. Train your eyes to always find what you gained even in failure. When you possess such a vision, you transcend the idea of failure and initiate the permanence of hope.

Failure is only a roadblock that reveals the path to take next time.

OCTOBER 21

STABILITY
Firmness in position; continuance without change

In nature, one of the most outstanding items to witness is the tallest tree in the world – the redwood. Another amazing sight is the largest mound in the world – Mount Everest. In order to reach amazing heights these spectacular sights had to possess a common trait – a vast, strong foundation. You also must aim to have sound fundamentals in every aspect of your life to build consistency into your daily regimen.

The greatest creation can only stand on the strongest foundation.

OCTOBER 22

MODESTY
The quality or state of being unassuming or moderate in the estimation of one's abilities

The healthy balance of modesty will keep you emotionally intact. Without confidence in yourself, you lack the tenacity to go for what you want. However, arrogance will isolate you from the people who have opportunities for you. Good and bad situations will fill your plate daily. Your modesty will help you increase the potential for more positive to occur then negative.

The higher the pedestal you put yourself on, the further you have to fall.

OCTOBER 23

PRUDENCE
Wise or judicious in practical affairs

Life has a very interesting quality when you actively seek to make proper decisions. It has the tendency to become simpler as you exhibit wise decision-making. Better decision-making will improve circumstances and situations when working to fulfill your purpose. Wisdom in application is a skill to be learned at any age. Envision what you want out of life then consider the good choices that will propel you there.

You can never go wrong when you are doing what is right.

OCTOBER 24

NEEDS
The lack of something wanted or deemed necessary

Our lives can become so flooded with society's version of what "should" be important to us that we misplace our priorities. Our needs are very few in number. Food, clothes, shelter, safety, education and love are the main things required externally. We, however, are responsible for filling the most important cognitive needs. Confidence, creativity, determination, persistence and selflessness all rest within our sphere of control. We will need every bit of them on our journey.

The need above all others is hope.

OCTOBER 25

PLEASURE
Enjoyment or satisfaction derived from what is to one's liking

You must be mindful of how you celebrate after your success has been reached. There is nothing at all wrong with doing or having what you enjoy as long as you do no harm to yourself or others. Your focus, however, is not to consume yourself with pleasures. Use moderation to balance your time and energy so you do not become a victim of your own satisfaction. Contentment can hinder your progress, if unchecked.

Do not allow the pleasures of the world to interrupt your purpose in the world.

OCTOBER 26

OPPORTUNITY
An appropriate or favorable time for attainment of a goal

Opportunities are the tools used on the path to your purpose. They can come in all shapes and sizes. Some opportunities may appear to require much time and energy to undertake. Others will arrive in a more subtle way. Nonetheless, they can all lead you to your goal. When you are overwhelmed, nervous or even afraid of an opportunity, attack with everything you got. You have been waiting this moment for a long time.

Frustration and hardships are signals that opportunities are approaching soon.

OCTOBER 27

BARRIERS
A circumstance or obstacle preventing communication or access

Sometimes you will hear the painful words of rejection. It is not the easiest thing to endure but you <u>will</u> recover. Opportunities will present themselves as long as you continue to work hard and learn the lessons along the way. You are getting closer when you begin to hit barriers. The more you hear "no", your quickly approaching the "yes". No matter what happens, you must continue to move forward.

When the doors of opportunity are shut in your face,
find the closest window.

OCTOBER 28

POPULARITY
Being known to the general public or particular group

Popularity is not a goal. Many people miss their purpose in life because they wanted be popular and accepted by the masses. Anyone can be popular, especially in these times. At its core, popularity is as simple as doing something outrageous for the sake of being shocking or controversial. Do not waste your time with being popular – strive to be significant. When you are significant you will mean something of irreplaceable value and will earn noble respect from others. Significance will always hold more value than popularity.

Aim to be meaningful, not to be popular.

OCTOBER 29

STUDY

Application of the mind to process information and acquire knowledge gained by reading, investigation or reflection

The best resources to learn about success are all around you and they are not limited to just a select few individuals. Everyone is successful in a particular way, even if he or she is unaware of the fact. Watch successful people and ask them questions about their experiences. How did they feel about the journey toward their accomplishment? What tools did they use? What hurdles did they overcome? This information will prove valuable in your development.

When you witness success, grab a pencil and paper.

OCTOBER 30

OBEDIENCE

Dutiful or submissive compliance

Obedience is essential when pursuing your purpose because sometimes you will have to dig deep to do what is essential for you to progress. If all goals were easy to attain, there would be no satisfaction achieving them because anyone would be able to do it. The factor that separates you from others is your level of discipline. Your discipline creates your consistency, which increases your performance, then denotes your high value. How much is your future worth?

Following wise instructions will keep you from common pitfalls.

OCTOBER 31

PURPOSE

Reason for which something is done, created or exists

Some believe that the journey to fulfill your singular purpose in life will take a lifetime. This sounds as though you only have one purpose, which is not true. Life is abundant and dynamic so all purposes are the catalysts for your life. One day, your purpose may be to teach someone how to read and instill within them the joy of education. Another moment you may be saving the life of a friend or complete stranger. Our purpose in life is not a mere statement of a lonely achievement, but rather a list of meaningful events, big and small, that made the difference in the lives of others.

Have you fulfilled your purposes today?

NOVEMBER

THE PURSUIT OF HAPPINESS

What makes you happy? Some people who have all that they desire are gravely unhappy, while others with very little possessions express the most happiness. How is this possible? True happiness is not connected to your circumstances, it is linked with your attitude toward the circumstances. Seek those things that give you fulfillment and happiness will come as a byproduct of your quest.

NOVEMBER 1

JUSTICE

The upholding of what is just, especially fair treatment and due reward in accordance with honor or standards

Justice is the most natural human condition. For justice to exist there must be order. Justice and order permeate every aspect of life because of the rules to which we adhere. Payment is the result of completed work for employment. Improved health is the result of consuming better quality food. The path to our happiness resides in the proper treatment of ourselves and others. Our actions contain benefits and consequences. The more we align in our actions to what is just, the more opportunities and benefits we receive.

Always seek to uphold what is right, fair and lawful.

NOVEMBER 2

HARMONY

Agreement in action or opinion; accord

Everything is comprised of parts that make up the whole. Vehicles, computers and other machinery can all be broken down into much simpler individual pieces to get a full understanding of the item. Our lives reflect the same pattern. Every area of our lives can be examined and improved. The better quality parts of a machine, the better the performance. In family, career, self-esteem, etc., as the quality of each improves, the more fulfilling life becomes. Consider each aspect of your life. What parts can you upgrade to make your existence better?

Harmony unfolds as you build inner peace.

NOVEMBER 3

APPEARANCE
The look or impression of someone or something

Strive to present yourself in a respectful way. Although the exterior is not the main determining factor, your appearance communicates to everyone where you have been and where you are going. Be very careful of judging the appearance of others because some people will lie. They will give an illusion of what they know you want to see so they can capitalize. To recognize these fictitious people, examine their actions and adherence to their word to find inconsistencies.

Do not place all value in appearance because the reality may differ from your visual expectation.

NOVEMBER 4

ABSENCE
An occasion or period of being away from a place or person.

Imagine walking along the beach on a sunny afternoon. You pass long stretches of sand, umbrellas and other vacationers. The atmosphere is pure paradise when compared to the intense work that happens in the common existence in the corporate world. The beach vacation for most of us is considered a major event because it happens so infrequently. Our interactions work the same way. Our lives influence those we contact. When we live a good life that stands out from others, our truth shines before us and the zest for a good life becomes infectious. We become the valuable targets for others to reach out to because they may find peace, understanding and resolution just by speaking with us.

The rare always has a higher value than the common.

NOVEMBER 5

POWER
Remarkable ability to do or act; might

A battery alone can do nothing. Even the largest battery is useless by itself. However, if you insert the battery into a mechanism serving a purpose, the energy can flow and be productive. For us to be productive, the cycle must begin by guiding our thoughts to create the energy to invoke action. These actions are the physical expressions of our power. To make things happen, you must take charge of your life.

What is the source of your power?

NOVEMBER 6

MODERATION
To be within reasonable limits; not excessive or extreme

Overindulgence is not the way to reach a happy place in your life. Some opportunities will come your way only to serve as an indicator of your degree of control. To engorge in yourself with all the available options at a buffet will only lead to an upset stomach. However, if you eat a balanced meal with proper portions, you can enjoy the culinary experience. In life, aspire for optimum balance and understand when enough is enough.

Too much of anything is never a good thing.

NOVEMBER 7

GLORY

Great honor, praise, or distinction accorded by common consent

Achievement is your primary focus. Greatness is your aim. Admiration will be bestowed upon you as you become more successful. Nothing extra needs to be done because you <u>earned</u> the praise. Unfortunately, you will encounter people who want the same glory without the hard work and dedication. Eventually, they will learn that accepting glory only comes after the shedding of sweat. Continue your work.

Beware those who seek glory. They will do <u>anything</u> to get it.

NOVEMBER 8

BLAME

To assign responsibility for a fault or wrong

Ask yourself a couple of questions before blaming others for your condition. First, did you have a choice in the matter causing your condition? What could have done to change your circumstances? If yes was the answer to either of those questions, it is time for reality check. No matter what others may do to you, it is your decision to accept it or not.

Being knocked down is not your fault; staying down is.

NOVEMBER 9

PACIFY
To ease the anger or agitation of

Your reading of this volume confirms that you are far beyond the need for infantile pacifiers. If people are only seeking to pacify you, let them know that the small band-aid is not sufficient to solve the large problem. Make them accountable for a solution to the problem by establishing specific conditions to be met by clear deadline. The laziness of a few people cannot hinder your progress.

*Do not accept a temporary quick-fix
when the problem is unresolved.*

NOVEMBER 10

FORTITUDE
Courage in pain or adversity

At the end of every disastrous moment, there will only be you. At the conclusion of every triumph, again, there will only be you at the end of the day. Your desired goals may be lofty and time consuming, yet you must possess a place to house your strength when times get tough. In this sacred place, you must shelter and guard three things: your vision, your action plan and your inspiration. Always keep them close because somewhere between now and your success, you will need them to give you the strength to finish.

*You must believe that you are capable and worthy
of achieving your goals set before you.*

NOVEMBER 11

HUMOR

The quality making something laughable or amusing

The best thing to do to cope with some situations is to laugh it off. Laughter is a natural stress reliever to help to curb your anger when dealing with stubborn people or immaturity. There is no time for you to become enraged over the occasional absurdity of others or even yourself. Sometimes, you must take a step back and have a good laugh in the midst of ridiculous events.

Laughter is the best medicine even when the joke is on you.

NOVEMBER 12

THOUGHTS

An idea or mental picture, imagined and contemplated

A thought is the immeasurable source of all things. Everything of the past, currently in existence and in the future shares the fact of originally being a thought before coming into fruition. All thoughts are the precursors to action. An action can change a nation; therefore, a thought can change the world. Your thoughts are so important that a seemingly insignificant thought to you can directly affect the generations of tomorrow. What thoughts can bring you closer to a state of happiness?

Manage your thoughts well - they will eventually become reality.

NOVEMBER 13

INTEGRITY

The quality of being honest and having strong moral principles

Some people, while on the path toward their achievements, will have no problem lying or wrongdoing others to get what they want. Do not feed into their ways because they clearly lack the key ingredient for lasting achievement: integrity. They do not understand or are ignoring the fact that they are destroying the relationship with those who would wholeheartedly support them. In due time, all of the wrongdoings will return to the surface.

Integrity is defined by what you do compared to what you say.

NOVEMBER 14

MATURITY

The state or quality of being fully-grown or developed

Physical maturity can be estimated to gauge when growth has occurred. Mental maturity is much more difficult to measure because age is a minor factor. The person's level of understanding is the featured characteristic. This is why there can be instances of a youth showing profound maturity while someone of substantial age can make such amateur decisions. To be wise is not to be equated with old age, rather, with sound decision-making and acceptance of responsibilities.

Some people grow older while others grow up.

NOVEMBER 15

REFINE

To improve by making small changes to make more accurate

In the cooking world, the more pure and refined the ingredients are, the higher the likelihood for a better quality meal. Every aspect of our being is an ingredient within our overall life. Are you making the best quality decisions from the available information and options? Are you experiencing thoughts of the anger or is despair clouding your vision? We all encounter days such as these. If you have not, keep living – they will come. These days are opportunities for your daily growth. Examine your life and change one thing for the better every day. You may be pleasantly surprised about who greets you in the mirror tomorrow.

Everyday is an opportunity to improve what you did yesterday.

NOVEMBER 16

PURITY

Freedom from contamination

Your happiness is not a mere place, rather, a state of mind. When maximizing your mental efforts, having a pure focus will allow you to think and work more efficiently. To attain this heightened purity of thought, you must instantly discard all doubt and negativity. Some of these impurities will come from others, however the overwhelming majority will come directly from you. Constructive criticism can build you up, however accepting negativity only will break you down. The better skilled you become at resisting the negativity, the more focus you can direct toward your goals.

To be pure of heart and mind helps to minimize the barriers of your success.

NOVEMBER 17

INTOXICATION

The physiological state produced by a poison or other toxic substance

Poisons, by definition, are hazardous and can be detrimental to your being. Ironically, some good things yield similar detrimental results if we allow them to change our values. For example, you win the lottery. Instead of being content, you want to show off and believe that you are better than the public because of your possessions. Such intoxication only leads to foolishness and will damage your relationships with others. Even the best things in life can be toxic to you if they are not managed well.

Plant your feet on solid ground to avoid having your head in the clouds.

NOVEMBER 18

LISTEN

To attend closely for the purpose of hearing

The wisest people often speak the least because they mastered the art of listening. Has someone ever asked for information from you, but would not stop talking long enough to hear your answer? Such instances are frustrating and unproductive experiences. To maximize the happiness in your life is a learning process. Some people have the questions, while others have the answers. Both sides are equally important. Idle chatter has no benefit. The less unproductive words you speak, the simpler your life will become.

Your ears are the gateway of wisdom.

NOVEMBER 19

PROTECTION

A person or thing preventing that prevents harm or injury

Your possessions are valuable whether you monetarily or emotionally invested in them. Unfortunately, some people are willing to steal your possessions instead of them getting their own. With such laziness and greed present, you must protect what is yours. Even with this being the case, on the other hand, some things in life must come to an end. The things that you once protected may be yours no more. You must release the physical and emotional tie so you accept the next great episode that life presents to you.

It is vital to protect what is yours, but more important to know when to let it go.

NOVEMBER 20

POTENTIAL

Qualities or abilities that may be developed and lead to future success

Happy people excel in the use of many skills yet one stands out in particular. They developed the gift of seeing the good from all situations. Fantastic things can come from both good and bad circumstances. You must develop your vision. What do you do when situations do not align with your plans? In stormy moments, do you interpret it as a bunch of dreary clouds sent to ruin your day or as the end of a devastating drought? Perspective makes all the difference.

There is always a strong chance for good things to happen.

NOVEMBER 21

AUTONOMY
Freedom to determine one's own actions

Venture out to seek your independence when you are fully prepared. Keep in mind that your independence will come with immense responsibility. For this reason, preparation is essential. Learn the necessary skills to operate independently and take pride in having your own domain to manage. Accumulate additions to your estate and wisely lend a helping hand to show others how to do the same.

Freedom of choice is the primary contributor to your happiness.

NOVEMBER 22

DEEDS
Something done, performed, or accomplished

Every action matters whether majestic or seemingly insignificant. Each deed performed is another mark in the timeline of your existence. Once you realize the importance placed on your actions, is easier to see the flaws in another's actions. The choices you make must honorably advance you in some fashion. Even though the temptation to achieve by deceitful means will always be present, it is never worth tarnishing your good name.

The fact that no one is perfect does not give you permission to deliberately make mistakes.

NOVEMBER 23

VARIETY
The quality or state of being different or diverse

If your happiness is based on having options, then trying a variety of experiences will give you more options from which to choose. There is nothing wrong with having a preference. When you, however, are open to new choices, you find new instances to inspire freshness and excitement in your life. Occasionally, if you find something not of your liking, at least you learned what to avoid for the next time.

Add variety to your life by trying new things.

NOVEMBER 24

ACQUIRE
To obtain an asset for oneself or to learn a skill, habit, or quality

Life as a whole can be seen as a series of learning experiences. More information gives us options to choose and pursue. We then can find out what is needed to accomplish the related goals. Upon completion of the tasks, we can understand what did and did not work for us. Next time, we can operate more efficiently. Throughout this entire process for achievement, we learn the specific skills and knowledge necessary to act resourcefully in the pursuit of our goals. Your tool belt will become heavier as you evolve.

The more things you own that free your time will add to your overall wealth.

NOVEMBER 25

SILENCE
Complete absence of sound

Moments will come when the circumstances of life will be overwhelming. There will be numerous deadlines to meet and some close relationships may be strained because of them. In order to cope with the stress, sometimes you must sit in silence. To go into a quiet room is not good enough. You must bring about peace within you. Calm your mind from racing and relax your emotions by focusing on a single positive aspect of your life. The time alone will allow you the moment of clarity to put everything into perspective and give you the energy you need to see your tasks through to completion.

Silence is the first step to meditate within chaotic situations.

NOVEMBER 26

CONFIDENCE
The feeling or belief that one can rely on someone or something

Your accomplishments begin and end with you. Between those two points will be friends to encourage you and people who will do or say anything to deter you from reaching your goals. You must always be confident in yourself. You can be successful in every venture you attempt. Even if you are temporarily unable to execute a certain task, remember, you always can learn what is needed and how to fulfill what is required of you for next time.

No one will believe in your greatness until you believe in it first.

NOVEMBER 27

RECREATION
Activity done for enjoyment when one is not working

When the work is done and the long day is over, you must treat yourself. The easiest way to burn out during periods of intense working sessions is to avoid playtime. This can be any assortment of activities you enjoy to give your mind and body a break from the pressures of productivity. Play a round of golf, read a long awaited novel from your favorite author or go for an evening walk. All of these are terrific outlets for you to partake. Take a moment to enjoy yourself.

After you work hard, be sure to you play hard.

NOVEMBER 28

PLANNING
To arrange a method or scheme beforehand for any work

Planning for success is one of the most underrated aspects to consider in regards to your goals. The three stages of success are learning, planning and performing. The planning stage serves as the bridge from abstract ideas to the concrete performance necessary to complete the desired tasks. Create your plan of action and envision each piece necessary to reach your goal. The more detailed your plan, the less adjustments will be required when unexpected events occur.

To reach your destination of joyous achievement,
follow a proven road map.

NOVEMBER 29

ACCEPTANCE

The action of consenting to receive or undertake something offered

If granted an abundance of choices to improve the quality of your life, what would you choose? We often think we do not deserve the whole pie, so we accept a little piece. The truth, however, is that we own the right to all the best quality things that life has to offer. Somewhere along the way, we settled and accepted this mediocre life. It is never too late to experience all that life has to offer. So, get out there and take command of your destiny.

Do not settle for less when you know you deserve better.

NOVEMBER 30

HAPPINESS

State of pleasure or blissful satisfaction

What is happiness? Is it found in possession of things? No. Is it found by having an abundance of relationships? No. Happiness is merely the joyful attitude upon accepting what is. Even if the accepted condition is not your preference, you can change the condition for the better or improve your outlook toward it. You cannot base your happiness on fickle things. This is like trying to build on sand. In consideration of all the positive and negative experiences, base your joy on the goodness of life. Hope for tomorrow is an essential component because happiness is created – it doesn't just happen.

The majestic view is seen only from a higher perspective.

DECEMBER

CONSTRUCTING YOUR FUTURE

Life is a series of plantings and harvests. To yield the most plentiful crops, you must envision success before the planting. Then you must act by creating the conditions that support the abundance you seek. Decide which direction you want your life to go and strive to reach each of your goals. It is your duty and responsibility to yourself and future generations to create your best life.

DECEMBER 1

ABILITY
The power or capacity to do or act

In order to control your desired future, you must take inventory of yourself. What past successes built your skills to where they are now? The question then becomes how you can take what you possess to get what you want. From your inventory of abilities, you must seek opportunities to challenge and stretch you beyond where you are currently. Have faith in your abilities and they will reward you in time.

Everyone has ability but the great ones know how and when to use them.

DECEMBER 2

ACTION
The process or state of performing a task

Throughout the course of life, we are constantly in a state of want. We may want a certain brand of clothes, the newest form of entertainment, or time to engage in our favorite hobbies. Wanting, however, is not enough when we consider the magnitude of our goals. Someone sitting idly can yearn for something for a long time, yet without actions to support desires, is guaranteed to produce nothing. Decide what all you want and pursue them now!

Life does not reward desire; it rewards action.

DECEMBER 3

TIME
The duration of an allotted or given period

Far beyond money and jewelry, there is one invaluable resource – time. Your wasted moments will never be experienced again. Your time is valuable because the world can be changed for the better in an instant. If the world can alter with such speed, then a nation can be unified through the people who choose to see life from a better perspective. Every moment, we must invest in the improvement of everything and everyone around us, since we will never know how much time remains.

Use your time wisely and efficiently because you will never see this moment again.

DECEMBER 4

FOCUS
To direct toward a particular point or purpose

Although you may be bombarded with various tasks, numerous meetings and countless deadlines, those who handle these responsibilities best understand the same secret – you can only do one thing at a time. Do not concern yourself with the enormous size of your task list. Prioritize your list and focus on one job to be completed at a given time. It is much better to finish your work properly than waste your resources repeating work to make the corrections.

Despite a mountain of distractions, you must have tunnel vision to accomplish your goal.

DECEMBER 5

CHOICES

An act of making a selection when faced
with two or more possibilities

Your destiny is inextricably tied to the choices that you make. Even when looking at where you are in life today, you are in this position because of a series of your prior choices. Redirect the compass of your decision-making if you want to change the path of your life. Do not rely solely on others to make your decisions for you. They are already managing their own life and cannot govern yours too. Choose the direction of your life and the world will get out of your way.

As your decision-making improves, so will your circumstances.

DECEMBER 6

REALITY

The quality or state of being actual or true

You must be careful when considering what is real and what is not. Some people will tell you all types of lies so you can do what they want you to do. This sounds horrible and deceitful, yet we do so much worse to ourselves. Always seek the absolute truth in every aspect of your life so you do not cause harm toward another person. Cultivate your ideas and energy in a truthful space. Your decisions and actions then will be justly fruitful.

Seek that which is genuine and true because it will last forever.

DECEMBER 7

PREDICT

To say or estimate that a specified thing will happen in the future or will be a consequence of something

Anticipation is a useful indicator of your growth and denotes the wisdom you have attained. The more you are able to take your past knowledge to envision what is to come, you will be able to avoid some of the many pitfalls experienced by those who act more recklessly and without foresight. As you lean on those consistent events and concepts, you will experience much more alignment between what to expect and what you actually receive.

Those who think ahead of situations are rarely caught off guard.

DECEMBER 8

ENLIGHTENMENT

The attainment of knowledge or insight

Life is merely a collection of journeys. We are given just enough resources to sustain ourselves, yet have boundless ability to pursue anything we desire. The most common link of humanity is the desire to live a good life. Each personal journey has the goal of maximizing the level of goodness in his or her life to be enjoyed. We all engage in the greater purpose to help each other reach and maintain the joy in life. To this end, as we assist others, we also create joy for ourselves.

Be better tomorrow than you are today.

DECEMBER 9

SACRIFICE

To surrender or give up, or permit injury or disadvantage to, for the sake of something else

You must make major sacrifices to accomplish your goals. Some of your favorite hobbies will be postponed. Socializing with your most intimate circles must also wait, even if relationships strain. There may be some nights where you are so engulfed in fulfilling your destiny that sleeping escapes you. Right now, you are assembling the building blocks of your future. Moments will come when you must make choices to sacrifice certain things because you believe in your goals. Your success will be worth the tough times.

To clear a space for your triumphs, some things must be let go.

DECEMBER 10

CRITICISM

The act of passing judgment or to find fault

You must be careful with what type of criticism you choose to accept. Constructive criticism informs you of your faults and suggest solutions for improvement. Destructive criticism is only given to discourage and break your spirits because it is derived from anger or resentment. Those who give you constructive criticism are the people to hold close to you. Their experience and candor will prove beneficial as you invest in the building of your future.

Accept criticism only from those qualified to give it.

DECEMBER 11

CHESS

A board game for two players with the objective of capturing or checkmating the opposing king

Chess is truly a metaphor for life. With a clearly defined objective in mind, you must strategize your moves by thinking ahead constantly. Along the way, you will encounter some situations when you may lose a piece of yourself. Patience and diligence empowers you to maximize all you have left to put yourself in the best position to win.

*Your victories will come from making
the right moves at the right time.*

DECEMBER 12

ILLUSIONS

A deceptive appearance or impression

Moments will arrive when you believe the lies before you. You sometimes will even shift your logic to give support to these lies. You will believe you are not good enough and this moment is as good as life is going to be. You will convince yourself that you are not capable of having other opportunities. These all are mere illusions designed to cloud your judgment and poison your self-esteem. You must decide to resist these lies. You are qualified and completely capable of having the positive and fruitful life you want to live.

*Do not be fearful of the successful person
you destined to become.*

DECEMBER 13

OPENNESS
Without obstructions to passage or view

The areas you have been exposed to will increase your available options. The more exposed you are, you gain a more broad perspective to apply to your life. For example, a person who has eaten only one type of food has a limited view of the culinary arts. However, if they become open to eating foods from other countries, they become more experienced and informed to make a greater scope of food choices. Your options are few when your experience is limited.

The more open you are to new experiences, the more opportunities will come your way.

DECEMBER 14

TRIBUTE
An act, statement, or gift intended to show gratitude or admiration

We often award people who accomplish outstanding things. It is just as important to give tribute to those who exhibit excellence in the consistency of their performance. This encouragement energizes the recipient to continue doing a job well done and teaches us how to identify the qualities that denote outstanding people. A good practice is to give tribute to those aimed at noble goals.

Praise the consistent as well as the extraordinary.

DECEMBER 15

OPTIMISM
Hopefulness and confidence about the future or
the successful outcome of something

It is easy to believe the best times of your life have already passed. Your best athletic times may have been when you were still in high school. You may think your marriage was perfect in the first couple of years. Those memories are not the pinnacle of your life. Your better days are always in front of you because as we learn and improve, our lives evolve beyond where we are. No matter what has happened to you in your past, tomorrow will always find a way to shine brighter than today.

The greatest benefits often come from the worst conditions.

DECEMBER 16

CERTAINTY
The quality of being reliably true and firm
conviction that something is the case

In the building of your future, many pivotal moments will be defined by your decision-making. Do your best to confirm the accuracy of your information by researching the topic in question. There is nothing worse than making important decisions based on the wrong information. Ask experts in the field to gain perspective, however, do not be bound by anyone's opinion because that can change in the blink of an eye.

Base your judgments on what IS true,
instead of what MAY be true.

DECEMBER 17

TRAVEL

Make a journey, typically of some length or abroad

Another key area of your development centers on the learning of various cultures aside from your own. The opportunity to travel across different parts of the world exposes you to cultures and norms unlike your own. This interaction opens your eyes to new customs of societies, yet there is one deeper level to consider – how similar we all are. Despite the location on earth, all of humanity shares an abundance of traits and ideas.

Learning of various cultures will help you to appreciate your life.

DECEMBER 18

INCREASE

Become or make greater in size, amount, intensity, or degree

One facet of productivity is to always maximize assets. The constant task before us is to use our resources in such a way that we strive to increase them. More resources allow us to care for our families more effectively and give charitably to those who are legitimately unable to work. This is the underlying reason why we must use our creativity more and celebrate those who already do. Those are the people who we can learn from so then we can improve our own process.

Strive to take what you have and multiply it.

DECEMBER 19

RESISTANCE

The refusal to accept or comply with something

People, at times, will take actions toward you or place conditions upon you to your detriment. You must remember that you own the right to stand up for yourself against anyone who tries harm you. No one has the power over you unless you give it to him or her. You are in charge of your life and must defend yourself at all costs so you have every opportunity to create the life you desire to live.

You have the power to resist all things that are not beneficial to you.

DECEMBER 20

PROGRESS

Forward or progression toward a destination

There will be moments when you feel stagnant while working toward your goals. It will seem as though the more work and energy you invest, when you look at the results, there is nothing happening. Nonetheless, you must keep going. There is always progress made when you look in the right places. Set smaller milestones along the way to your goal and celebrate your progress.

ANY progress is always better than NO progress.

DECEMBER 21

TOMORROW
The day after today

One of the biggest mistakes you can make is to base your future solely according to your past. The past is nothing more than an assortment of memories and lessons. The time that absolutely affects your future is your now. Each present act and thought will directly affect tomorrow. To become an expert musician, you must begin practicing right now. Consider your life goals and energize your now to begin creating your desires for tomorrow.

Work today and plan tentatively for tomorrow.

DECEMBER 22

TIMING
The choice, judgment, or control of when something should be done

Timing is everything. The equation of success can be interpreted as Success = Position + Timing. Most often, we only focus on doing a enough work to put ourselves in the right position but we don't consider the importance of timing. When we feel as though we are ready, we tend to force things to happen when we want them to occur. This can be just as detrimental because even though we may possess exactly what we want, we did not learn how to maintain the triumph. If we learn to prepare and patiently wait for the opportunity, the success will be long-lasting.

Life becomes more challenging when there is a magnificent occurrence at the wrong time.

DECEMBER 23

CHANCE
Do something by accident or without design

Many people pursuing success find themselves believing that their hope for an opportunity is a matter of chance. They declare that only those with good luck will be successful. Every occurrence in the world is a result of collective energy and action. Learn what is needed and work toward recognizing opportunities. When the opportunities arrive, expect to gain success when you perform. You did not "luck" into success - you earn the achievement.

There is no such thing as coincidence.

DECEMBER 24

PATIENCE
The capacity to accept or tolerate delay, trouble, or suffering without getting angry or upset

Understand and accept the fact that as long as you are working toward goals, there will always be much work to do. You will carry a long list of tasks and, as your ambition grows, you will continually add to your list. Nonetheless, do not overwhelm yourself. You have time. You will be more efficient as you work diligently and with a patient state of mind. If you rush, your emotions can stifle your thinking and restrict proper decision-making. This causes you to overlook key areas of your work. Manage your time well to avoid the temptation to rush.

The journey toward success is traveled only one task at a time.

DECEMBER 25

FREEDOM
The state of being unrestricted rather than in confinement or under physical restraint

Your quality of life is based on the level of freedom you possess. What is freedom? How do you know when you have attained such sovereignty? Those who are truly free have mastered all fear. Every illusion is based in fear. When you consider what you may be afraid of and realize your power to overcome it, you find liberation from fears' paralyzing affects. You then can allow your energy to circulate into productive actions to pursue your goals.

Exercise the liberty to make any fruitful decision in your life.

DECEMBER 26

PERFECTION
The condition, state, or quality of being free or as free as possible from all flaws or defects

Seeking perfection may be rooted in good intentions; however, it can lead to frustration and a waste of resources. Such faultlessness is often based on the opinion of another person's ideal concept or performance. Rather than setting perfection as the measurement of success, consider quality. Humanity is not perfect. We may encounter positive and negative experiences, yet at the end of the day, our overall experience of life is good. Anytime we have an opportunity to improve the quality of our lives, it is surely a good thing.

Perfection may not exist, but high quality does.

DECEMBER 27

REFLECTION

A mirrored image, representation or counterpart

We often dislike looking at ourselves in the mirror. We analyze ourselves with intense criticism of pointing out each of our unbearable flaws. With time, we become angry and bitter at ourselves for who we "think" we are. In contrast, what could happen if we began to view ourselves with constructive criticism? We start by accepting ourselves for who we are and set goals for our improvement. Life is about doing the best we can with our resources and believing in the power we possess. When looking in the mirror, we must appreciate the terrific person who is there.

Your reflection displays the symbol of limitless possibilities.

DECEMBER 28

TECHNOLOGY

The application of scientific knowledge for practical purposes in industry, machinery and equipment developed from such knowledge

As humanity progresses, ideas and inventions will flourish. New technology allows people to share concepts and improve processes for achieving a greater amount of complete work in a much shorter a lot of time. Use this to your advantage. Proper use of technology allows you to work much more efficiently and give you the opportunity to be innovative within your tasks. Your ambition and available technology will always complement each other well.

Maximize the resources that save you time and energy.

DECEMBER 29

INFINITE
Unlimited extent of time, space, or quantity; boundlessness

The mind is the beginning of all dreams because your goals must start in a clear, boundless space. In this space, there are infinite possibilities to plant the seed of your dreams. As your positive thoughts and education nourish the seedling, energy is being created which causes you to take your idea into the physical world without regard of any limitations. With time, such a plant will become a deeply rooted tree allowing you to take your success and branch out into other areas of success.

Your dreams should be just as abundant as your imagination.

DECEMBER 30

LEGACY
Something handed down from an ancestor or from the past

Whether intentional or not, your life will leave a legacy with others. Within this moment, you are not only orchestrating your future to influence your family and others close to you - you are building THE future. The influence you can have on the world is outstanding. All of this depends on the manner in which you live your life. How do you want to be known and remembered? When you arrive at the answer, live your life in such a way that your actions align well with your decision. This generation and others are waiting to hear about you.

How will your page affect the book of humanity?

DECEMBER 31

DETERMINATION

A firm and resolute movement towards some object or end

The opportunities for success are all around you. How hard will you work to attain them? All of that is left up to you. All barriers are temporary and you must decide on how your life will unfold. Once that decision is made, the fluidity of life will bend as you wish. With the billions of people in the world, only one person is needed to change it for the better. Your personal success can be the catalyst for the improvement of all humanity. With your determination, nothing is impossible.

Fate cannot deny the destiny of the determined soul.

THE TRUTH

Your personal revolution to live your best life does not end here - it actually begins. After careful and sincere examination to master your True Self, your Connections and your Power, you still may wonder *"Am I truly that powerful?"* or *"Can I really create the life that I want?"* The answer to both is a resounding YES, however, there is an ultimate decision needed that only you can make. You must decide to be motivated and inspired to work toward your goals to make your life worth living. You are the only person empowered to carry this torch of achievement to live your best life.

During this noble pursuit, you are kindling the flames of PEACE – **Personal Enlightenment And Constant Evolution**. Therefore, PEACE is not a destination – it is a philosophy. It is a way of looking at the greatness within yourself and the world to yield the most positive outcome for your journey through life. Although the road may be challenging at times, you must learn productive techniques and apply sound principles to constantly improve yourself. As you evolve, you become a beacon of hope that others will model themselves after and they, too, will improve their lives and circumstances.

Through such strength and influence, you are much more powerful that you can ever imagine. The world is simply a testing ground for you to prove your worthiness and resolve but you must hold fast to the principles of self-confidence, conflict resolution and everlasting hope to lead you through another day. Use this wisdom to encourage a deeper understanding about yourself and how to better manage life.

Let every day greet you with joy and confidence as you live your dreams one moment at a time. Live a life of fulfillment and uplift others along the way. There are over 7 billion people on Earth, yet it only takes one person to change the world for the better. The truth is that there is no question of whether you have the ability to live your best life to bring peace to the world. Where there is a doubt of your power, there is the illusion of fear. However, where there is declaration of the greatness within you, there is certainty. Where there is certainty, there is **PEACE**.

YOU ARE THE ONE